THE PYTHON CODE WARRIOR

WARRIOR

Doing Access With Gusto!

By Richard Thomas Edwards

This is the Dedicated to all my friends I left behind and never got a chance to say goodbye.

CONTENTS

THE PURPOSE OF THIS BOOK

You can learn a lot in a short time when you have the basics
that you know already works.
—R. T. Edwards

W hen I started working on this book, I thought I had a
pretty good handle on what I knew I could or couldn't
do with Access. After all, I did work for Microsoft in
Technical Support between 1996 and 2002 and many of the issues I
worked on were dealing with Access 2, 95, 97 and 2000. But today's
Office 365 is a beast! It has more horsepower and more bells and
whistles than ever before!

But not all of Access's enhancements are Internet "tribal
knowledge".

In fact, I can promise you that some solutions will be found only
here because a lot of the issues are being caused by Microsoft's
once respected MSDN – on or not on purpose – that just do not
work, are vague, misleading and have code examples that are
VB.Net prejudicial – they are written for PowerShell, C# or C++.Net.

Why in the world would a company who has devoted the last 25 years to using the Component Object Model (COM) not want to embrace languages and encourage the use of Perlscript, Python, Rexx and Ruby. If the excuse is that they think these languages should go away, they aren't any time soon. Which is one of the many reasons why I chose to learn Python in the first place. After all, languages were built to address a problem or groups of problems that couldn't be solved using existing and popular programming languages.

What I'm about to cover is the newest version of Access: Access 365; and, hopefully amaze you with brilliant solutions you won't find on the web.

SO WHY AN E-BOOK ON ACCESS

Better than an out of the box experience.

Knowing what is possible and what you are capable of, makes you a code champion.
—R. T. Edwards

L et's face it, out of the box solutions are boring often supplied to fuel your imagination. Unfortunately, many programmers just don't have the time to spend learning how and why the pieces of the puzzle do, indeed, work with each other to generate something bigger and better than the program was designed to do out of the box.

My goal here is to take work out the kinks – so to speak – and supply you with the solutions and the work arounds. The result: saving you time effort and tons of frustration in the process.

SO, WHAT IS SO GREAT ABOUT THE DOM

Master the DOM, save the world.
—R. T. Edwards

L isten, I don't plan on making you an overnight success But if you've gotten this far into this book, then what I'm about to cover will make up for all the time you have spent so far to get here. Imagine for a moment, having to write code blindfolded.

Wouldn't be easy, would take a lot longer to do and you probably wouldn't get paid much in the process. Well, the DOM is like your eyes into the object that you create in code. And in the case of Access it is a rather large inventory of things to do and stuff to add to your Python code.

For example, you go up to the web and they tell you that using Access.Application, you can write the following to create an Access database:

```
import win32com.client

oAccess = win32com.client.Dispatch("Access.Application")
```

```
oAccess.NewCurrentDatabase(DBName, 9) #For an Access 2000
database

oAccess = win32com.client.Dispatch("Access.Application")
oAccess.NewCurrentDatabase(DBName, 10) #For an Access 2002
database


oAccess = win32com.client.Dispatch("Access.Application")
oAccess.NewCurrentDatabase(DBName, 12) #For an Access 2007
database

oAccess = win32com.client.Dispatch("Access.Application")
oAccess.NewCurrentDatabase(DBName, 0) #For creating a
Default Access database
```

Furthermore, not all the DOMs for the various versions of Access are the same. For example – I believe it is the Access DOM for 2007 – which also had support for Access 2, Access 95 and Access 97 – would have allowed you to do all the above and these three:

```
oAccess = win32com.client.Dispatch("Access.Application")
oAccess.NewCurrentDatabase(DBName, 1) #For an Access 2
database

oAccess = win32com.client.Dispatch("Access.Application")
oAccess.NewCurrentDatabase(DBName, 7) #For an Access 95
database

oAccess = win32com.client.Dispatch("Access.Application")
oAccess.NewCurrentDatabase(DBName, 8) #For an Access 97
database
```

But that is not as important as the fact that the compatible DAO suggests some other rather important and interesting database creation formats of its own:

```
dbVersion10    1
dbVersion11    8
dbVersion20    16
dbVersion30    32
dbVersion40    64
dbVersion120   128
dbVersion140   256
dbVersion150   512
```

Only problem is, these additional versions are not in COM. In fact, the COM or Component Object Model engine installed on the machine I am typing this on is DAO.DBEngine.120. I seriously doubt that you're going to get dbVersion140 or dbVersion150 out of DAO.DBEngine.120.

But this book isn't about DAO. That will get covered in a different E-book. Right now, we're going to be dealing with Access and the Access.Application object we can call from COM.

ANOTHER CRITICAL SUBJECT

The Import\export functionality in Access

Never assume you think you know how to do something. When
you don't, it will bite you in the butt every time.
—R. T. Edwards

The first thing you need to know about this is I am taking what I know about it and fixing an issue that even Microsoft's MSDN's explanation of it is so misleading that you couldn't possibly get it to work. Please, look at the following code:

```
l = win32com.client.Dispatch("WbemScripting.SWbemLocator")
svc = l.ConnectServer(".", "root\\cimv2")
svc.Security_.AuthenticationLevel = 6
svc.Security_.ImpersonationLevel = 3
ob = svc.Get("" + TBLName + "")
objs = ob.Instances_
```

```
oAccess = win32com.client.Dispatch("Access.Application")
oAccess.NewCurrentDatabase("D:\Process.accdb", 0)
db = oAccess.CurrentDB()
tbldef = db.CreateTableDef("Process_Properties")
For obj in objs:
    For prop in obj.Properties_:
        fld = tblDef.CreateField(rs.Fields[x].Name, 12)
        fld.AllowZeroLength = True
        tbldef.Fields.Append(fld)

    break

db.tableDefs.Append(tbldef)
rs = db.OpenRecordset("Process_Properties")
For obj in objs:
    rs.AddNew
    For prop in obj.Properties_:
        n= rs.Fields[x].Name
        rs.Fields(n).Value = GetValue(n, obj)

    rs.Update
```

When this code is finished it will create an Access Database with an accdb file extension.

But suppose I wanted to Export the file into a text file?
If could write the following:

```
cn = win32com.client.Dispatch ("ADODB.Connection")
```

```
cn.ConnectionString ="Provider=Microsoft.Jet.OLEDB.4.0;Data
Source = D:\Process.accdb;"
cn.Open

cn.Execute("Select * INTO[Text; hdr=yes; Format=CSVDelimited;
Database=D:\].[Process_Properties.csv] From [Products]")
```

Or, I could do this:

```
oAccess = win32com.client.Dispatch("Access.Application")
oAccess.OpenCurrentDatabase("D:\Process.accdb")
oAccess.DoCmd.TransferText 2,"","Process_Properties",
"D:\Process1.csv",1,,437
```

All well and good but what happens if I don't want a CSV file format? Perhaps a tilde or Exclamation?

As it turns out, there is a bit of Magic you do.

Start Access, open the database you want to use for exporting, highlight the table you want to export and then right click it.

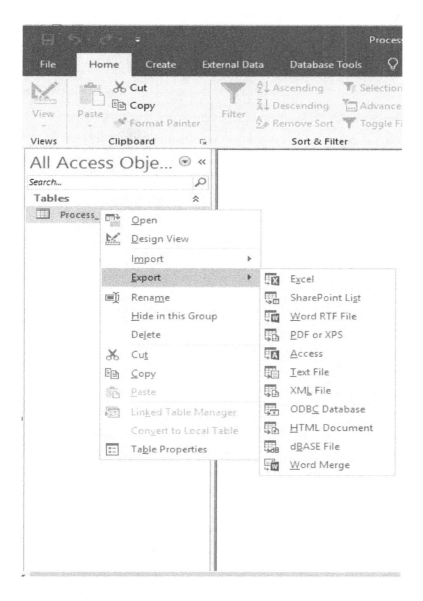

Slide down the list to Text File and click it.

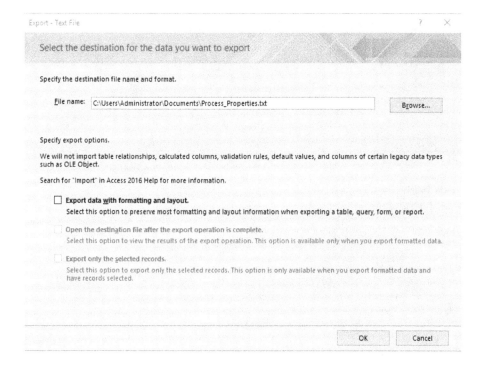

Other than placing the file in a different location besides the default location, click Okay.

If you select the Export data with formatting and layout, you will not get to the next important step. Change the location, leave everything else alone.

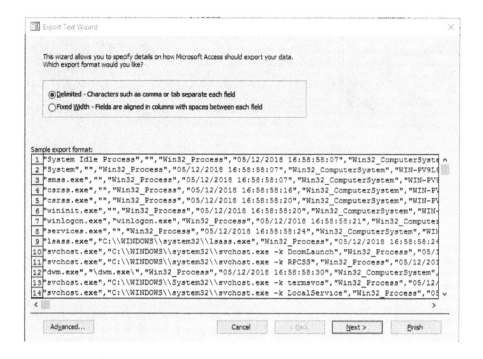

If you've worked with Excel before, this might look kind of familiar. Anyway, the next step is to click on the Advanced button on the left.

That will bring you to where you master the craft of importing and exporting.

First, change the delimiter in the Combo box right beside the Field Delimiter label. Do not click okay. Instead, click on the Save As button. The program will go through the list of field names and create an input dialog where you can change the name pf the Specification file.

Either write it down the name provided or change it to a name you want to use.

Click okay.

Congratulations! You now have your specification file Name!

Now, click the okay.

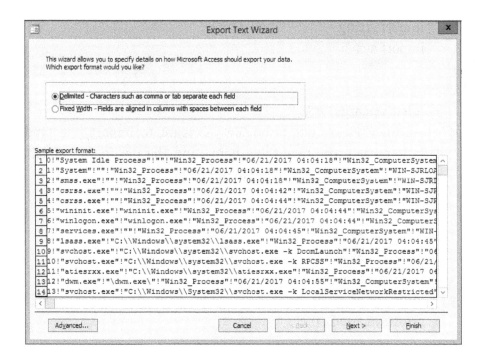

Notice the delimiter you selected has replaced the comma . The file will be created after you click finish.

You have now created your first custom delimited file.

The problem as I see it is all of this is very user specific and, in all honesty, not programmer friendly. Let's put the control back into the programmer's hands.

We're going to need four arguments for both the input and output files:

Since the first one is the name of the script we're creating, what we want is the name of the source file, the type of delimiter we're dealing with and the name of the destination database.

```
import win32com.client
import string
import sys



if len(sys.argv) < 5:
    print ("Please enter the file you want to import, the type of delimiter used, the new table name and the destination database where you want the new table to be added.")
    quit()

print(sys.argv[0])
print(sys.argv[1])
print(sys.argv[2])
print(sys.argv[3])
print(sys.argv[4])
```

Forgetting the delimiter:

C:\Users\Administrator>C:\Users\Administrator\Desktop\args.py C:\Greattimes.txt Products D:\Process.accdb
Please enter the file you want to import, the type of delimiter used, the new table name and the destination database where you want the new table to be added.

Adding the delimiter:

C:\Users\Administrator>C:\Users\Administrator\Desktop\args.py
C:\Greattimes.txt ~ Products D:\Process.accdb
C:\Users\Administrator\Desktop\args.py
C:\Greattimes.txt

~

Products
D:\Process.accdb

Continuing with the code:

```
import win32com.client
import sys


if len(sys.argv) < 5:
    print ("Please enter the file you want to import, the type of
delimiter used, the new table name and the destination database
where you want the new table to be added.")
    quit()

#source = sys.argv[1]
#d = sys.argv[2]
#tbln = sys.argv[3]
#dest = sys.argv[4]

#for testing the code
source = "C:\Products.csv"
d = ","
tbln = "Products"
dest = "D:\Process.accdb"
```

```
cnstr                    =                    "Provider=MSDASQL;Extended
Properties=\"Driver={Microsoft Text Driver (*.txt; *.csv)}; hdr=yes;
format=Delimited(d); dbq=C:\\;\";"
    print(cnstr)
    rs1 = win32com.client.Dispatch("ADODB.Recordset")
    rs1.ActiveConnection = cnstr
    rs1.Cursorlocation = 3
    rs1.LockType =3
    rs1.Open("Select * from [Products.csv]")

    oAccess = win32com.client.Dispatch("Access.Application")
    oAccess.OpenCurrentDatabase("D:\Process.accdb")
    db = oAccess.CurrentDB()
    tbldef = db.CreateTableDef(tbln)
    for x in range(rs1.Fields.Count):
      fld = tbldef.CreateField(rs1.Fields(x).Name, 12)
      fld.AllowZeroLength = True
      tbldef.Fields.Append(fld)

    db.TableDefs.Append(tbldef)

    rs = db.OpenRecordset("Products")
    while rs1.eof == False:
      rs.AddNew()
      for x in range(rs1.Fields.Count):
        rs.Fields(x).Value = rs1.Fields(x).Value

      rs.Update()
      rs1.MoveNext()
```

The result:

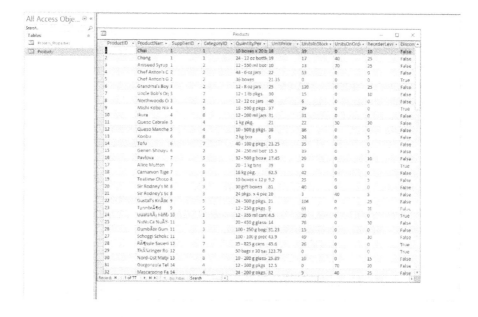

Now, let's go the other way. We want to export:

```
import win32com.client
import string
import sys


#if len(sys.argv) < 5:
#    print ("Please enter the file you want to import, the type of
delimiter used, the new table name and the destination database
where you want the new table to be added.")
#    quit()


#source = sys.argv[1]
#d = sys.argv[2]
#tbln = sys.argv[3]
#dest = sys.argv[4]
```

```python
#for testing the code
source = "D:\\Process.accdb"
d = "!"
tbln = "Process_Properties"
dest = "C:\\Process.txt"
tempstr = ""


oAccess = win32com.client.Dispatch("Access.Application")
oAccess.OpenCurrentDatabase(source)
db = oAccess.CurrentDB()

ws = win32com.client.Dispatch("WScript.Shell")
fso = win32com.client.Dispatch("Scripting.FileSystemObject")
txtstream = fso.OpenTextFile(dest, 2, True, -2)

rs = db.OpenRecordset(tbln)
for x in range(rs.Fields.Count):
    if tempstr != "":
        tempstr = tempstr + d

    tempstr = tempstr + rs.Fields[x].Name
txtstream.WriteLine(tempstr)
tempstr =""
while rs.EOF == False:
    for x in range(rs.Fields.Count):
        if tempstr != "":
            tempstr = tempstr + d

        tempstr = tempstr + '"' + str(rs.Fields[x].value) + '"'
    txtstream.WriteLine(tempstr)
```

```
    tempstr = ""
    rs.MoveNext()

txtstream.Close()
```

And the result:

```
Process - Notepad                                    —    □    ×

File  Edit  Format  View  Help

Caption!CommandLine!CreationClassName!CreationDate!CSCreationClas ^
"System Idle Process"!""!"Win32_Process"!"05/12/2018 16:58:58:07"
"System"!""!"Win32_Process"!"05/12/2018 16:58:58:07"!"Win32_Compu
"smss.exe"!""!"Win32_Process"!"05/12/2018 16:58:58:07"!"Win32_Com
"csrss.exe"!""!"Win32_Process"!"05/12/2018 16:58:58:16"!"Win32_Co
"csrss.exe"!""!"Win32_Process"!"05/12/2018 16:58:58:20"!"Win32_Co
"wininit.exe"!""!"Win32_Process"!"05/12/2018 16:58:58:20"!"Win32_
"winlogon.exe"!"winlogon.exe"!"Win32_Process"!"05/12/2018 16:58:5
"services.exe"!""!"Win32_Process"!"05/12/2018 16:58:58:24"!"Win32
"lsass.exe"!"C:\\WINDOWS\\system32\\lsass.exe"!"Win32_Process"!"0
"svchost.exe"!"C:\\WINDOWS\\system32\\svchost.exe -k DcomLaunch"!
"svchost.exe"!"C:\\WINDOWS\\system32\\svchost.exe -k RPCSS"!"Win3
"dwm.exe"!"\dwm.exe\"!"Win32_Process"!"05/12/2018 16:58:58:30"!"W
"svchost.exe"!"C:\\WINDOWS\\System32\\svchost.exe -k termsvcs"!"W
"svchost.exe"!"C:\\WINDOWS\\system32\\svchost.exe -k LocalService
"svchost.exe"!"C:\\WINDOWS\\System32\\svchost.exe -k LocalService
"svchost.exe"!"C:\\WINDOWS\\System32\\svchost.exe -k LocalSystemN
"svchost.exe"!"C:\\WINDOWS\\system32\\svchost.exe -k NetworkServi
"svchost.exe"!"C:\\WINDOWS\\system32\\svchost.exe -k LocalService
"NVDisplay.Container.exe"!"\C:\\Program Files\\NVIDIA Corporation
"svchost.exe"!"C:\\WINDOWS\\system32\\svchost.exe -k netsvcs"!"Wi
"WUDFHost.exe"!"\C:\\Windows\\System32\\WUDFHost.exe\ -HostGUID:1
380"!"0"!"0"
"svchost.exe"!"C:\\WINDOWS\\system32\\svchost.exe -k LocalService
"svchost.exe"!"C:\\WINDOWS\\System32\\svchost.exe -k NetworkServi
"svchost.exe"!"C:\\WINDOWS\\System32\\svchost.exe -k LocalService
"svchost.exe"!"C:\\WINDOWS\\System32\\svchost.exe -k smbsvcs"!"Wi
"spoolsv.exe"!"C:\\WINDOWS\\System32\\spoolsv.exe"!"Win32_Process
"svchost.exe"!"C:\\WINDOWS\\system32\\svchost.exe -k apphost"!"Wi
                                                                 v
<                                                                >
```

So, now, we have two totally customized Python scripts which enable importing and exporting files to Access. The rest of our export functions will be based on connecting to Access and enumerating through what we've created

THE ACCESS CODE

The routines being used in the book

Creating forms, writing code in VBScript is not something you want to do if you are a Python programmer. I know I wouldn't. So, with that in mind, this book is staying out of the internal workings of what Access does and connecting to Access to connect or create databases, create and populate tables and establish connections with recordsets we want to use to display information. We will be creating:

- ASP
- ASPX
- Attribute XML
- Colon Delimited Text Files
- Comma Delimited Text Files
- Element XML
- Element XML For XSL
- Exclamation Delimited Text Files
- Excel Automation
- Excel Spreadsheet
- Excel using a CSV File
- HTA

- HTML
- Schema XML
- Semi Colon Delimited File
- Tab Delimited File
- Tilde Delimited File
- XSL Files

With that said, it is time to look at the way this e-book uses Access and after that, we will start building code from those routines.

THE SOURCE CODE

Programming for effect

*You can't write code without knowing the building blocks
needed to write it.*
—R. T. Edwards

There is nothing more important than knowing what the code is doing to get the job done. How can you fix an issue with it if you can't find the issue? One of the reasons why I was good at solving customers' issues was because I was able to look at the code and could spot the problem.

With that thought freshly in your mind, since we are dealing with a Database and a recordset, we can use the field names for our headers and the field values for our data.

But we start with this first:

```
import win32com.client
import string

oAccess = win32com.client.Dispatch("Access.Application")
```

```
oAccess.OpenCurrentDatabase(DBName)
db = oAccess.CurrentDB()
rs = db.OpenRecordset(TBLName)
```

At this point, we shouldn't have to write this continually. However, because we are writing code as separate entities, you will see the above code in each one.

Next comes writing out the header routines. Technically, creating XML files is the only place where we break the mould. The first routine below is used with the almost dozen Delimited file examples

```
for x in range(rs.Fields.Count):
  if tempstr != "":
    tempstr = tempstr + d

  tempstr = tempstr + rs.Fields[x].Name
txtstream.WriteLine(tempstr)
tempstr =""
```

And for everything except XML:

```
txtstream.WriteLine("<tr>")
for x in range(rs.Fields.Count):
  txtstream.WriteLine("<th>" + rs.Fields[x].Name + "</th>")

txtstream.WriteLine("</tr>")
```

After that, you're going to find the same routine sandwiched between the rs row enumerator:

```
while rs.EOF == False:
    for x in range(rs.Fields.Count):
            if tempstr != "":
                    tempstr = tempstr + d

    tempstr = tempstr + '"' + str(rs.Fields[x].value) + '"'
    txtstream.WriteLine(tempstr)
    tempstr =""
    rs.MoveNext()
```

```
while rs.EOF == False:
    txtstream.WriteLine("<tr>")
    for x in range(rs.Fields.Count):
        txtstream.WriteLine("<td>"  +  str(rs.Fields[x].Value)  +
"</td>")

    txtstream.WriteLine("</tr>")
    rs.MoveNext()
```

As for XML:

```
while rs.EOF == False:
    txtstream.WriteLine("<" + TBLName + ">")
    for x in range(rs.Fields.Count):
```

```
    txtstream.WriteLine("<" + rs.Fields[x].Name + ">" +
str(rs.Fields[x].Value) + "</" + rs.Fields[x].Name + ">")

    txtstream.WriteLine("</" + TBLName + ">")
    rs.MoveNext()
```

When doing vertical rendering of ASP, ASPX, HTA, HTML and delimited text files you will see this:

```
  for x in range(rs.Fields.Count):
    txtstream.WriteLine("<tr><th>" + rs.Fields[x].Name +
"</th>")
    rs.MoveFirst()
    while rs.EOF == False:
      txtstream.WriteLine("<td>" + str(rs.Fields[x].Value) +
"</td>")

    rs.MoveNext()
    txtstream.WriteLine("</tr>")
```

And that pretty much covers all of the routines we're going to be using throughout the rest of this book.

CREATING ASP WEBPAGES USING ACCESS

ASP may be old school, but it still works.
—R. T. Edwards

he stylesheets you can use with ASP, ASPX, HTA, HTML and XSL are at the end of this e-book. I could add them to each one of these chapters, but some are so long that adding them would just add more and more pages to this book and even I don't like the concept of having page after page of stylesheet code for every example I write.

```
import win32com.client
import string

oAccess = win32com.client.Dispatch("Access.Application")
oAccess.OpenCurrentDatabase(DBName)
db = oAccess.CurrentDB()
rs = db.OpenRecordset(TBLName)
```

```
ws = win32com.client.Dispatch("WScript.Shell")
fso = win32com.client.Dispatch("Scripting.FileSystemObject")

txtstream           =           fso.OpenTextFile(ws.CurrentDirectory           +
"\Product.asp", 2, true, -2)
```

Single Line Horizontal View

```
txtstream.WriteLine("<html
xmlns=""http://www.w3.org/1999/xhtml"">")
txtstream.WriteLine("<head>")
txtstream.WriteLine("<title>" + TBLName + "</title>")
txtstream.WriteLine("<body>")
txtstream.WriteLine("<table     border=""1""     colspacing=""3""
colpadding=""3"">")
txtstream.WriteLine("<%")

txtstream.WriteLine("Response.Write(""<tr>"" + vbcrlf) ")
For x in range(rs.Fields.Count):
     txtstream.WriteLine("Response.Write(""<th>"                    +
rs.Fields[x].Name + "</th>"" + vbcrlf)")

txtstream.WriteLine("Response.Write(""</tr>"" + vbcrlf)")
txtstream.WriteLine("Response.Write(""<tr>"" + vbcrlf) ")
For x in range(rs.Fields.Count):
     value = rs.Fields[x].value
     txtstream.WriteLine("Response.Write(""<td>"   +   value   +
"</td>"" + vbcrlf)")

txtstream.WriteLine("Response.Write(""</tr>"" + vbcrlf)")
rs.MoveNext()
```

```
txtstream.WriteLine("%>")
txtstream.WriteLine("</table>")
txtstream.WriteLine("</body>")
txtstream.WriteLine("</html>")
txtstream.Close()
```

Multi Line Horizontal view

```
txtstream.WriteLine("<html
xmlns=""http://www.w3.org/1999/xhtml"">")
txtstream.WriteLine("<head>")
txtstream.WriteLine("<title>" + TBLName + "</title>")
txtstream.WriteLine("<body>")
txtstream.WriteLine("<table border=""1"" colspacing=""3""
colpadding=""3"">")
txtstream.WriteLine("<%")


txtstream.WriteLine("Response.Write(""<tr>"" + vbcrlf) ")
For x in range(rs.Fields.Count):
    txtstream.WriteLine("Response.Write(""<th>"           +
rs.Fields[x].Name + "</th>"" + vbcrlf)")

txtstream.WriteLine("Response.Write(""</tr>"" + vbcrlf)")
rs.MoveFirst()
While rs.EOF = false:
    txtstream.WriteLine("Response.Write(""<tr>"" + vbcrlf) ")
    For x in range(rs.Fields.Count):
        value = rs.Fields[x].value
        txtstream.WriteLine("Response.Write(""<td>"  +  value  +
"</td>"" + vbcrlf)")
```

```
    txtstream.WriteLine("Response.Write(""</tr>""" + vbcrlf)")
    rs.MoveNext()


  txtstream.WriteLine("%>")
  txtstream.WriteLine("</table>")
  txtstream.WriteLine("</body>")
  txtstream.WriteLine("</html>")
  txtstream.Close()
```

Single Line Vertical View

```
  txtstream.WriteLine("<html
xmlns=""http://www.w3.org/1999/xhtml"">")
  txtstream.WriteLine("<head>")
  txtstream.WriteLine("<title>" + TBLName + "</title>")
  txtstream.WriteLine("<body>")
  txtstream.WriteLine("<table    border=""1""    colspacing=""3""
colpadding=""3"">")
  txtstream.WriteLine("<%")


  For x in range(rs.Fields.Count):
      txtstream.WriteLine("Response.Write(""<tr><th>"         +
rs.Fields[x].Name + "</th>""" + vbcrlf)")
      txtstream.WriteLine("Response.Write(""<td>"             +
str(rs.Fields[x].value)  + "</td></tr>""" + vbcrlf)")


  txtstream.WriteLine("%>")
  txtstream.WriteLine("</table>")
```

```
txtstream.WriteLine("</body>")
txtstream.WriteLine("</html>")
txtstream.Close()
```

Multi Line Vertical View

```
txtstream.WriteLine("<html
xmlns=""http://www.w3.org/1999/xhtml"">")
txtstream.WriteLine("<head>")
txtstream.WriteLine("<title>" + TBLName + "</title>")
txtstream.WriteLine("<body>")
txtstream.WriteLine("<table    border=""1""    colspacing=""3""
colpadding=""3"">")
txtstream.WriteLine("<%")


For x in range(rs.Fields.Count):
    txtstream.WriteLine("Response.Write(""<tr><th>"          +
rs.Fields[x].Name + "</th>""" + vbcrlf)")
rs.MoveFirst()
While rs.EOF = false:
        txtstream.WriteLine("Response.Write(""<td>"          +
value + "</td>""" + vbcrlf)")
        rs.MoveNext()

    txtstream.WriteLine("Response.Write(""</tr>""" + vbcrlf)")


txtstream.WriteLine("%>")
txtstream.WriteLine("</table>")
```

```
txtstream.WriteLine("</body>")
txtstream.WriteLine("</html>")
txtstream.Close()
```

BUILDING ASPX WEBPAGES FROM ACCESS

elow is the code needed to create an aspx file.

B

```
import win32com.client
import string

oAccess = win32com.client.Dispatch("Access.Application")
oAccess.OpenCurrentDatabase(DBName)
db = oAccess.CurrentDB()
rs = db.OpenRecordset(TBLName)

ws = win32com.client.Dispatch("WScript.Shell")
fso = win32com.client.Dispatch("Scripting.FileSystemObject")
txtstream  =  fso.OpenTextFile(ws.CurrentDirectory  +  "\\"  +
TBLName + ".aspx", 2, True, -2)
```

Single Line Horizontal View

```
    txtstream.WriteLine("<!DOCTYPE html PUBLIC \"-//W3C//DTD
XHTML 1.0 Transitional//EN\"
\"http://www.w3.org/TR/xhtml1/DTD/xhtml1-transitional.dtd\">")
    txtstream.WriteLine("<html
xmlns=\"http://www.w3.org/1999/xhtml\">")
    txtstream.WriteLine("<head>")
    txtstream.WriteLine("<title>" + TBLName + "</title>")
    txtstream.WriteLine("<body>")
    txtstream.WriteLine("<table    border=""1""    colspacing=""3""
colpadding=""3"">")
    txtstream.WriteLine("<%")

    txtstream.WriteLine("Response.Write(""<tr>""" + vbcrlf) ")
    For x in range(rs.Fields.Count):
        txtstream.WriteLine("Response.Write(""<th>"              +
rs.Fields[x].Name + "</th>""" + vbcrlf)")

    txtstream.WriteLine("Response.Write(""</tr>""" + vbcrlf)")
    txtstream.WriteLine("Response.Write(""<tr>""" + vbcrlf) ")
    For x in range(rs.Fields.Count):
        value = rs.Fields[x].value
        txtstream.WriteLine("Response.Write(""<td>"   +   value   +
"</td>""" + vbcrlf)")

    txtstream.WriteLine("Response.Write(""</tr>""" + vbcrlf)")
    rs.MoveNext()

    txtstream.WriteLine("%>")
    txtstream.WriteLine("</table>")
    txtstream.WriteLine("</body>")
    txtstream.WriteLine("</html>")
    txtstream.Close()
```

Multi Line Horizontal view

```
    txtstream.WriteLine("<!DOCTYPE html PUBLIC \"-//W3C//DTD
XHTML 1.0 Transitional//EN\"
\"http://www.w3.org/TR/xhtml1/DTD/xhtml1-transitional.dtd\">")
    txtstream.WriteLine("<html
xmlns=\"http://www.w3.org/1999/xhtml\">")
    txtstream.WriteLine("<head>")
    txtstream.WriteLine("<title>" + TBLName + "</title>")
    txtstream.WriteLine("<body>")
    txtstream.WriteLine("<table    border=""1""    colspacing=""3""
colpadding=""3"">")
    txtstream.WriteLine("<%")

    txtstream.WriteLine("Response.Write(""<tr>"" + vbcrlf) ")
    For x in range(rs.Fields.Count):
        txtstream.WriteLine("Response.Write(""<th>"                +
rs.Fields[x].Name + "</th>"" + vbcrlf)")

    txtstream.WriteLine("Response.Write(""</tr>"" + vbcrlf)")
    rs.MoveFirst()
    While rs.EOF = false:
      txtstream.WriteLine("Response.Write(""<tr>"" + vbcrlf) ")
      For x in range(rs.Fields.Count):
        value = rs.Fields[x].value
        txtstream.WriteLine("Response.Write(""<td>"   +   value   +
"</td>"" + vbcrlf)")

      txtstream.WriteLine("Response.Write(""</tr>"" + vbcrlf)")
      rs.MoveNext()
```

```
txtstream.WriteLine("%>")
txtstream.WriteLine("</table>")
txtstream.WriteLine("</body>")
txtstream.WriteLine("</html>")
txtstream.Close()
```

Single Line Vertical View

```
txtstream.WriteLine("<!DOCTYPE html PUBLIC \"-//W3C//DTD
XHTML 1.0 Transitional//EN\"
\"http://www.w3.org/TR/xhtml1/DTD/xhtml1-transitional.dtd\">")
txtstream.WriteLine("<html
xmlns=\"http://www.w3.org/1999/xhtml\">")
txtstream.WriteLine("<head>")
txtstream.WriteLine("<title>" + TBLName + "</title>")
txtstream.WriteLine("<body>")
txtstream.WriteLine("<table    border=""1""    colspacing=""3""
colpadding=""3"">")
txtstream.WriteLine("<%")

For x in range(rs.Fields.Count):
        txtstream.WriteLine("Response.Write(""<tr><th>"        +
rs.Fields[x].Name + "</th>""" + vbcrlf)")
        txtstream.WriteLine("Response.Write(""<td>"            +
str(rs.Fields[x].value)  + "</td></tr>""" + vbcrlf)")

txtstream.WriteLine("%>")
txtstream.WriteLine("</table>")
txtstream.WriteLine("</body>")
txtstream.WriteLine("</html>")
txtstream.Close()
```

Multi Line Vertical View

```
    txtstream.WriteLine("<!DOCTYPE html PUBLIC \"-//W3C//DTD
XHTML 1.0 Transitional//EN\"
\"http://www.w3.org/TR/xhtml1/DTD/xhtml1-transitional.dtd\">")
    txtstream.WriteLine("<html
xmlns=\"http://www.w3.org/1999/xhtml\">")
    txtstream.WriteLine("<head>")
    txtstream.WriteLine("<title>" + TBLName + "</title>")
    txtstream.WriteLine("<body>")
    txtstream.WriteLine("<table    border=""1""    colspacing=""3""
colpadding=""3"">")
    txtstream.WriteLine("<%")


    For x in range(rs.Fields.Count):
        txtstream.WriteLine("Response.Write(""<tr><th>"          +
rs.Fields[x].Name + "</th>""" + vbcrlf)")
    rs.MoveFirst()
    While rs.EOF = false:
            txtstream.WriteLine("Response.Write(""<td>"           +
value + "</td>""" + vbcrlf)")
            rs.MoveNext()

        txtstream.WriteLine("Response.Write(""</tr>""" + vbcrlf)")

    txtstream.WriteLine("%>")
    txtstream.WriteLine("</table>")
    txtstream.WriteLine("</body>")
    txtstream.WriteLine("</html>")
```

```
txtstream.Close()
```

BUILDING HTA FILES USING ACCESS

elow is the code needed to create an HTA File:

B

```
import win32com.client
import string

oAccess = win32com.client.Dispatch("Access.Application")
oAccess.OpenCurrentDatabase(DBName)
db = oAccess.CurrentDB()
rs = db.OpenRecordset(TBLName)

ws  = Win32com.client.Dispatch("WScript.Shell")
txtstream       =       fso.OpenTextFile(ws.CurrentDirectory   +
"\Products.html", 2, true, -2)
```

For Single Line Horizontal

```
txtstream.WriteLine("<html>")
txtstream.WriteLine("<head>")
```

```
txtstream.WriteLine("<HTA:APPLICATION ")
txtstream.WriteLine("ID = \"Products\" ")
txtstream.WriteLine("APPLICATIONNAME = \"Products\" ")
txtstream.WriteLine("SCROLL = \"yes\" ")
txtstream.WriteLine("SINGLEINSTANCE = \"yes\" ")
txtstream.WriteLine("WINDOWSTATE = \"maximize\">")
txtstream.WriteLine("<title>Products</title>")
'add a stylesheet here
txtstream.WriteLine("</head>")
txtstream.WriteLine("<body>")
txtstream.WriteLine("<table     Border='1'     cellpadding='1'
cellspacing='1'>")
txtstream.WriteLine("<tr>")
For x in range(rs.Fields.Count):
    txtstream.WriteLine("<th>" + rs.Fields[x].Name + </th>")

txtstream.WriteLine("</tr>")
txtstream.WriteLine("<tr>")
rs.MoveFirst()
For x in range(rs.Fields.Count):
    txtstream.WriteLine("<td>"    +    str(rs.Fields[x].value)    +
"</td>")

txtstream.WriteLine("</tr>")

txtstream.WriteLine("</table>")
txtstream.WriteLine("</body>")
txtstream.WriteLine("</html>")
txtstream.close()
```

For Multi Line Horizontal

```
txtstream.WriteLine("<html>")
txtstream.WriteLine("<head>")
txtstream.WriteLine("<HTA:APPLICATION ")
txtstream.WriteLine("ID = \"Products\" ")
txtstream.WriteLine("APPLICATIONNAME = \"Products\" ")
txtstream.WriteLine("SCROLL = \"yes\" ")
txtstream.WriteLine("SINGLEINSTANCE = \"yes\" ")
txtstream.WriteLine("WINDOWSTATE = \"maximize\">")
txtstream.WriteLine("<title>Products</title>")

'add a stylesheet here
txtstream.WriteLine("</head>")
txtstream.WriteLine("<body>")
txtstream.WriteLine("<table      Border='1'      cellpadding='1'
cellspacing='1'>")

txtstream.WriteLine("<tr>")
For x in range(rs.Fields.Count):
    txtstream.WriteLine("<th>" + rs.Fields[x].Name + </th>")

txtstream.WriteLine("</tr>")
rs.MoveFirst()
while rs.EOF == false:
    txtstream.WriteLine("<tr>")
    For x in range(rs.Fields.Count):
        txtstream.WriteLine("<td>"    +    str(rs.Fields[x].value)
+"</td>")

    txtstream.WriteLine("</tr>")
    rs.MoveNext()
```

```
txtstream.WriteLine("</table>")
txtstream.WriteLine("</body>")
txtstream.WriteLine("</html>")
txtstream.close()
```

For Single Line Vertical

```
txtstream.WriteLine("<html>")
txtstream.WriteLine("<head>")
txtstream.WriteLine("<HTA:APPLICATION ")
txtstream.WriteLine("ID = \"Products\" ")
txtstream.WriteLine("APPLICATIONNAME = \"Products\" ")
txtstream.WriteLine("SCROLL = \"yes\" ")
txtstream.WriteLine("SINGLEINSTANCE = \"yes\" ")
txtstream.WriteLine("WINDOWSTATE = \"maximize\">")
txtstream.WriteLine("<title>Products</title>")
'add a stylesheet here
txtstream.WriteLine("</head>")
txtstream.WriteLine("<body>")
txtstream.WriteLine("<table     Border='1'     cellpadding='1'
cellspacing='1'>")


    For x in range(rs.Fields.Count):
        txtstream.WriteLine("<tr><th>"    +    rs.Fields[x].Name    +
</th>")
        txtstream.WriteLine("<td>"    +    rs.Fields[x].Name    +
"</td></tr>")

    txtstream.WriteLine("</table>")
```

```
txtstream.WriteLine("</body>")
txtstream.WriteLine("</html>")
txtstream.close()
```

For Multi Line Vertical

```
txtstream.WriteLine("<html>")
txtstream.WriteLine("<head>")
txtstream.WriteLine("<HTA:APPLICATION ")
txtstream.WriteLine("ID = \"Products\" ")
txtstream.WriteLine("APPLICATIONNAME = \"Products\" ")
txtstream.WriteLine("SCROLL = \"yes\" ")
txtstream.WriteLine("SINGLEINSTANCE = \"yes\" ")
txtstream.WriteLine("WINDOWSTATE = \"maximize\">")
txtstream.WriteLine("<title>Products</title>")

'add a stylesheet here
txtstream.WriteLine("</head>")
txtstream.WriteLine("<body>")
txtstream.WriteLine("<table    Border='1'    cellpadding='1'
cellspacing='1'>")


For x in range(rs.Fields.Count):
    txtstream.WriteLine("<tr><th>"  +  rs.Fields[x].Name  +
</th>")
    while rs.EOF == False:
        txtstream.WriteLine("<td>"  +  str(rs.Fields[x].value)  +
"</td>")
        rs.MoveNext()
```

```
txtstream.WriteLine("</tr>")

txtstream.WriteLine("</table>")
txtstream.WriteLine("</body>")
txtstream.WriteLine("</html>")
txtstream.close()
```

BUILDING HTML FILES USING ACCESS

Below is the code needed to create an HTML File:

```
import win32com.client
import string

oAccess = win32com.client.Dispatch("Access.Application")
oAccess.OpenCurrentDatabase(DBName)
db = oAccess.CurrentDB()
rs = db.OpenRecordset(TBLName)

ws  = Win32com.client.Dispatch("WScript.Shell")
txtstream       =       fso.OpenTextFile(ws.CurrentDirectory    +
"\Products.html", 2, true, -2)
```

For Single Line Horizontal

```
txtstream.WriteLine("<html>")
txtstream.WriteLine("<head>")
txtstream.WriteLine("<title>Products</title>")
'add a stylesheet here
txtstream.WriteLine("</head>")
```

```
txtstream.WriteLine("<body>")
txtstream.WriteLine("<table      Border='1'      cellpadding='1'
cellspacing='1'>")

txtstream.WriteLine("<tr>")
For x in range(rs.Fields.Count):
    txtstream.WriteLine("<th>" + rs.Fields[x].Name + </th>")

txtstream.WriteLine("</tr>")
txtstream.WriteLine("<tr>")
rs.MoveFirst()
For x in range(rs.Fields.Count):
    txtstream.WriteLine("<td>" + rs.Fields[x].value+ "</td>")

txtstream.WriteLine("</tr>")
txtstream.WriteLine("</table>")
txtstream.WriteLine("</body>")
txtstream.WriteLine("</html>")
txtstream.close()
```

For Multi Line Horizontal

```
txtstream.WriteLine("<html>")
txtstream.WriteLine("<head>")
txtstream.WriteLine("<title>Products</title>")
'add a stylesheet here
txtstream.WriteLine("</head>")
txtstream.WriteLine("<body>")
txtstream.WriteLine("<table      Border='1'      cellpadding='1'
cellspacing='1'>")
txtstream.WriteLine("<tr>")
For x in range(rs.Fields.Count):
```

```
        txtstream.WriteLine("<th>" + rs.Fields[x].Name + </th>")

    txtstream.WriteLine("</tr>")
    rs.MoveFirst()
    while rs.EOF == false:
        txtstream.WriteLine("<tr>")
        For x in range(rs.Fields.Count):
            txtstream.WriteLine("<td>"      +      str(rs.Fields[x].value)
+"</td>")

        txtstream.WriteLine("</tr>")
        rs.MoveNext()


    txtstream.WriteLine("</table>")
    txtstream.WriteLine("</body>")
    txtstream.WriteLine("</html>")
    txtstream.close()
```

For Single Line Vertical

```
    txtstream.WriteLine("<html>")
    txtstream.WriteLine("<head>")
    txtstream.WriteLine("<title>Products</title>")
    'add a stylesheet here
    txtstream.WriteLine("</head>")
    txtstream.WriteLine("<body>")
    txtstream.WriteLine("<table      Border='1'      cellpadding='1'
cellspacing='1'>")
    For x in range(rs.Fields.Count):
```

```
        txtstream.WriteLine("<tr><th>"    +    rs.Fields[x].Name    +
</th>")
        txtstream.WriteLine("<td>"    +    rs.Fields[x].Name    +
"</td></tr>")


    txtstream.WriteLine("</table>")
    txtstream.WriteLine("</body>")
    txtstream.WriteLine("</html>")
    txtstream.close()
```

For Multi Line Vertical

```
    txtstream.WriteLine("<html>")
    txtstream.WriteLine("<head>")
    txtstream.WriteLine("<title>Products</title>")
    'add a stylesheet here
    txtstream.WriteLine("</head>")
    txtstream.WriteLine("<body>")
    txtstream.WriteLine("<table    Border='1'    cellpadding='1'
cellspacing='1'>")
    For x in range(rs.Fields.Count):
        txtstream.WriteLine("<tr><th>"    +    rs.Fields[x].Name    +
</th>")
        while rs.EOF == False:
            txtstream.WriteLine("<td>"    +    str(rs.Fields[x].value)    +
"</td>")
            rs.MoveNext()

    txtstream.WriteLine("</tr>")

    txtstream.WriteLine("</table>")
    txtstream.WriteLine("</body>")
```

```
txtstream.WriteLine("</html>")
txtstream.close()
```

CREATING TEXT FILES
FROM ACCESS

When you think outside of the box, you live beyond the world
of normal programming and become an innovator.
—R. T. Edwards

T ext files are databases, too. You just need to know how to
make them and what applications can use them to get the
most from them. Below are some of the most common
ones used today:

Access and Colon Delimited

```
import win32com.client
import string
```

```
oAccess = win32com.client.Dispatch("Access.Application")
oAccess.OpenCurrentDatabase(DBName)
  db = oAccess.CurrentDB()
  rs = db.OpenRecordset(TBLName)
  ws = Win32com.client.Dispatch("WScript.Shell")
     fso =
Win32com.client.Dispatch("Scripting.FileSystemObject)txtstrea
m = fso.OpenTextFile(ws.CurrentDirectory + "\Products.txt",
2, true, -2)
For x in range(rs.Fields.Count):
  if(strNames != ""):
    strNames = strNames + ":"

  strNames = strNames + rs.Fields[x].Name

txtstream.WriteLine(strNames)
rs.MoveFirst()
While rs.EOF = false:
  For x in range(rs.Fields.Count):
    if(strValues != ""):
      strValues= strValues + ":"

    strValues= strValue + "\"" + str(rs.Fields[x].value) + "\""

  txtstream.WriteLine(strValues)
  strValues= ""
  rs.MoveNext()
```

Access And Comma Delimited

```
import win32com.client
import string

oAccess = win32com.client.Dispatch("Access.Application")
oAccess.OpenCurrentDatabase(DBName)
db = oAccess.CurrentDB()
rs = db.OpenRecordset(TBLName)



ws  = Win32com.client.Dispatch("WScript.Shell")
fso = Win32com.client.Dispatch("Scripting.FileSystemObject)
txtstream        =        fso.OpenTextFile(ws.CurrentDirectory        +
"\Products.csv", 2, true, -2)

For x in range(rs.Fields.Count):
   if(strNames != ""):
      strNames = strNames + ","

   strNames = strNames + rs.Fields[x].Name

txtstream.WriteLine(strNames)
rs.MoveFirst()
While rs.EOF = false:
   For x in range(rs.Fields.Count):
      if(strValues != ""):
         strValues= strValues + ","

      strValues= strValue + "\"" + rs.Fields[x].value+ "\""

   txtstream.WriteLine(strValues)
   strValues= ""
   rs.MoveNext()
```

Access and Exclamation Delimited Code

```
import win32com.client
import string

oAccess = win32com.client.Dispatch("Access.Application")
oAccess.OpenCurrentDatabase(DBName)
db = oAccess.CurrentDB()
rs = db.OpenRecordset(TBLName)


ws = Win32com.client.Dispatch("WScript.Shell")
fso = Win32com.client.Dispatch("Scripting.FileSystemObject)
txtstream    =    fso.OpenTextFile(ws.CurrentDirectory    +
"\Products.txt", 2, true, -2)

For x in range(rs.Fields.Count):
    if(strNames != ""):
        strNames = strNames + "!"

    strNames = strNames + rs.Fields[x].Name

txtstream.WriteLine(strNames)
rs.MoveFirst()
While rs.EOF = false:
```

```
    For x in range(rs.Fields.Count):
        if(strValues != ""):
            strValues= strValues + "!"

        strValues= strValue + "\"" + rs.Fields[x].value+ "\""

    txtstream.WriteLine(strValues)
    strValues= ""
    rs.MoveNext()
```

Access and Semi-colon Delimited


```
import win32com.client
import string

oAccess = win32com.client.Dispatch("Access.Application")
oAccess.OpenCurrentDatabase(DBName)
db = oAccess.CurrentDB()
rs = db.OpenRecordset(TBLName)


ws  = Win32com.client.Dispatch("WScript.Shell")
fso = Win32com.client.Dispatch("Scripting.FileSystemObject)
txtstream       =       fso.OpenTextFile(ws.CurrentDirectory    +
"\Products.txt", 2, true, -2)

    For x in range(rs.Fields.Count):
        if(strNames != ""):
            strNames = strNames + ";"
```

```
        strNames = strNames + rs.Fields[x].Name

txtstream.WriteLine(strNames)
rs.MoveFirst()
While rs.EOF = false:
    For x in range(rs.Fields.Count):
        if(strValues != ""):
            strValues= strValues + ";"

        strValues= strValue + "\"" + rs.Fields[x].value+ "\""

    txtstream.WriteLine(strValues)
    strValues= ""
    rs.MoveNext()
```

Access And Tab Delimited

```
import win32com.client
import string

oAccess = win32com.client.Dispatch("Access.Application")
oAccess.OpenCurrentDatabase(DBName)
db = oAccess.CurrentDB()
rs = db.OpenRecordset(TBLName)


ws  = Win32com.client.Dispatch("WScript.Shell")
fso = Win32com.client.Dispatch("Scripting.FileSystemObject)
txtstream       =       fso.OpenTextFile(ws.CurrentDirectory    +
"\Products.txt", 2, true, -2)
```

```
For x in range(rs.Fields.Count):
    if(strNames != ""):
        strNames = strNames + vbtab

    strNames = strNames + rs.Fields[x].Name

txtstream.WriteLine(strNames)
rs.MoveFirst()
While rs.EOF = false:
    For x in range(rs.Fields.Count):
        if(strValues != ""):
            strValues= strValues + vbtab

        strValues= strValue + "\"" + rs.Fields[x].value+ "\""

    txtstream.WriteLine(strValues)
    strValues= ""
    rs.MoveNext()
```

Access And Tilde Delimited

```
import win32com.client
import string

oAccess = win32com.client.Dispatch("Access.Application")
oAccess.OpenCurrentDatabase(DBName)
db = oAccess.CurrentDB()
rs = db.OpenRecordset(TBLName)

ws  = Win32com.client.Dispatch("WScript.Shell")
fso = Win32com.client.Dispatch("Scripting.FileSystemObject)
```

```
txtstream        =      fso.OpenTextFile(ws.CurrentDirectory     +
"\Products.txt", 2, true, -2)

For x in range(rs.Fields.Count):
  if(strNames != ""):
    strNames = strNames + "~"

  strNames = strNames + rs.Fields[x].Name

txtstream.WriteLine(strNames)
rs.MoveFirst()
While rs.EOF = false:
  For x in range(rs.Fields.Count):
    if(strValues != ""):
      strValues= strValues + "~"

    strValues= strValue + "\"" + rs.Fields[x].value+ "\""

  txtstream.WriteLine(strValues)
  strValues= ""
  rs.MoveNext()
```

WORKING WITH EXCEL

The Tail of three ways to do it

I harbor the belief that the hardest thing a Python program should have to do is learn how to fly his or her private jet and enjoy life.

I'm not saying that the code I am providing here is going to get you there. What I am saying is the e-books that I am writing will certainly be a step in the right direction.

With that said, there are three ways to get information into excel:

Excel Automation

HORIZONTAL VIEW

```
import win32com.client
```

```
import string

oAccess = win32com.client.Dispatch("Access.Application")
oAccess.OpenCurrentDatabase(DBName)
db = oAccess.CurrentDB()
rs = db.OpenRecordset(TBLName)
oExcel  = Win32com.client.Dispatch("Excel.Application")
oexcel.Visible = True

wb = oExcel.Workbooks.Add()
ws = wb.WorkSheets(1)
ws.Name = "Products"
  x=1
y=2
for z = 0 to rs.Fields.Count-1
   ws.Cells.Item(1, x) = rs.Fields(z).Name
   x=x+1

x=1
rs.MoveFirst()
Do While rs.EOF = false
   for z = 0 to rs.Fields.Count-1
      ws.Cells.Item(y, x) = rs.Fields(z).value
      x=x+1

   x=1
   y=y+1
   rs.MoveNext()

ws.Columns.HorizontalAlignment = -4131
iret = ws.Columns.AutoFit()
```

```
import win32com.client
import string

oAccess = win32com.client.Dispatch("Access.Application")
oAccess.OpenCurrentDatabase(DBName)
db = oAccess.CurrentDB()
rs = db.OpenRecordset(TBLName)

oExcel – Win32com.client.Dispatch("Excel.Application")
oexcel.Visible = True

wb = oExcel.Workbooks.Add()
ws = wb.WorkSheets(1)
ws.Name = "Products"
x=1
y=2
for z = 0 to rs.Fields.Count-1
  ws.Cells.Item(x, 1) = rs.Fields(z).Name
  x=x+1

x=1
rs.MoveFirst()
Do While rs.EOF = false
  for z = 0 to rs.Fields.Count-1
    ws.Cells.Item(x, y) = rs.Fields(z).value
    x=x+1

  x=1
  y=y+1
  rs.MoveNext()
```

```
ws.Columns.HorizontalAlignment = -4131
iret = ws.Columns.AutoFit()
```

The last way is through an old time favorite, a physical spreadsheet:

Excel Spreadsheet

```
import win32com.client
import string

oAccess = win32com.client.Dispatch("Access.Application")
oAccess.OpenCurrentDatabase(DBName)
db = oAccess.CurrentDB()
rs = db.OpenRecordset(TBLName)


ws = win32com.client.Dispatch("WScript.Shell")
cdir = ws.CurrentDirectory + "\Process.xml"
fso                                         =
newWin32com.client.Dispatch("Scripting.FileSystemObject")
txtstream = fso.OpenTextFile(cdir, 2, true, -2)
txtstream.WriteLine("<?xml version=""1.0""?>")
txtstream.WriteLine("<?mso-application
progid=""Excel.Sheet""?>")
txtstream.WriteLine("<Workbook        xmlns=""urn:schemas-
microsoft-com:office:spreadsheet""      xmlns:o=""urn:schemas-
microsoft-com:office:office""  xmlns:x=""urn:schemas-microsoft-
com:office:excel""              xmlns:ss=""urn:schemas-microsoft-
```

```
com:office:spreadsheet""
xmlns:html=""http://www.w3.org/TR/REC-html40"">")
    txtstream.WriteLine("  <ExcelWorkbook xmlns=""urn:schemas-
microsoft-com:office:excel"">")
    txtstream.WriteLine("
<WindowHeight>11835</WindowHeight>")
    txtstream.WriteLine("
<WindowWidth>18960</WindowWidth>")
    txtstream.WriteLine("
<WindowTopX>120</WindowTopX>")
    txtstream.WriteLine("
<WindowTopY>135</WindowTopY>")
    txtstream.WriteLine("
<ProtectStructure>False</ProtectStructure>")
    txtstream.WriteLine("
<ProtectWindows>False</ProtectWindows>")
    txtstream.WriteLine("  </ExcelWorkbook>")
    txtstream.WriteLine("  <Styles>")
    txtstream.WriteLine("        <Style ss:ID=""s62"">")
    txtstream.WriteLine("            <Borders/>")
    txtstream.WriteLine("                <Font ss:FontName=""Calibri""
x:Family=""Swiss""    ss:Size=""11""    ss:Color=""#000000""
ss:Bold=""1""/>")
    txtstream.WriteLine("        </Style>")
    txtstream.WriteLine("        <Style ss:ID=""s63"">")
    txtstream.WriteLine("            <Alignment
ss:Horizontal=""Left""                ss:Vertical=""Bottom""
ss:Indent=""2""/>")
    txtstream.WriteLine("            <Font
ss:FontName=""Verdana""   x:Family=""Swiss""   ss:Size=""7.7""
ss:Color=""#000000""/>")
    txtstream.WriteLine("        </Style>")
```

```python
    txtstream.WriteLine(" </Styles>")
    txtstream.WriteLine("  <Worksheet ss:Name="""" + TBLName +
""""">")
    txtstream.WriteLine("<Table          x:FullColumns=""""1""""
x:FullRows=""""1"""" ss:DefaultRowHeight=""""24.9375"""">")
    txtstream.WriteLine("      <Column    ss:AutoFitWidth=""""1""""
ss:Width=""""82.5"""" ss:Span=""""5""""/>")
    txtstream.WriteLine("  <Row ss:AutoFitHeight=""""0"""">")
      For x in range(rs.Fields.Count):
        txtstream.WriteLine("<Cell       ss:StyleID=""""s62""""><Data
ss:Type=""""String"""">" + rs.Fields[x].Name + "</Data></Cell>")

    txtstream.WriteLine(" </Row>")
    rs.MoveFirst()
    While rs.EOF = false:
      txtstream.WriteLine("  <Row ss:AutoFitHeight=""""0"""">")
      For x in range(rs.Fields.Count):
        value = rs.Fields[x].value
        txtstream.WriteLine("     <Cell  ss:StyleID=""""s63""""><Data
ss:Type=""""String"""">" + value + "</Data></Cell>")

      txtstream.WriteLine(" </Row>")
      rs.MoveNext()

    txtstream.WriteLine("</Table>")
    txtstream.WriteLine("  </Worksheet>")
    txtstream.WriteLine("</Workbook>")
    txtstream.Close
```

Using A CSV File

```
import win32com.client
import string

oAccess = win32com.client.Dispatch("Access.Application")
oAccess.OpenCurrentDatabase(DBName)
db = oAccess.CurrentDB()
rs = db.OpenRecordset(TBLName)


ws  = Win32com.client.Dispatch(" WScript.Shell")
fso = Win32com.client.Dispatch("Scripting.FileSystemObject")

txtstream      =    fso.OpenTextFile(ws.CurrentDirectory    +
"\Products.xml", 2, true, -2)
   For x in range(rs.Fields.Count):
      if(strNames != ""):
         strNames = strNames + ";"

      strNames = strNames + rs.Fields[x].Name

   txtstream.WriteLine(strNames)
   rs.MoveFirst()
   While rs.EOF = false:
      For x in range(rs.Fields.Count):
         if(strValues != ""):
            strValues= strValues + ";"

         strValues= strValue + "\"" + rs.Fields[x].value+ "\""

      txtstream.WriteLine(strValues)
```

```
        strValues= ""
        rs.MoveNext()
```

....

VERTICAL VIEW

```
import win32com.client
import string

oAccess = win32com.client.Dispatch("Access.Application")
oAccess.OpenCurrentDatabase(DBName)
db = oAccess.CurrentDB()
rs = db.OpenRecordset(TBLName)


ws  = Win32com.client.Dispatch(" WScript.Shell")
fso  = Win32com.client.Dispatch("Scripting.FileSystemObject")

txtstream        =      fso.OpenTextFile(ws.CurrentDirectory     +
"\Products.xml", 2, true, -2)
    For x in range(rs.Fields.Count):
        strValues = rs.Fields[x].Name
        rs.MoveFirst()
        While rs.EOF = false:
            if(strValues != ""):
                strValues= strValues + ";"

            strValues= strValues + '"' + rs.Fields[x].value + '"'
            rs.MoveNext()

        txtstream.WriteLine(strValues)
        strValues= ""
```

```
txtstream.Close
ws.Run(ws.CurrentDirectory + "\Products.csv")
```
The last line will open your new file up in Excel.

CREATING XML FILES

Attribute XML

I may not be rich, but my children are my biggest asset.
—R. T. Edwards

What is attribute XML? This one always gets me in hot water. Why?

Because, technically any element formatted XML could also be considered Attribute XML with an Element tag. Technically, Attribute XML is one or more name and values contained within a single node.

```
import win32com.client
import string

    oAccess = win32com.client.Dispatch("Access.Application")
    oAccess.OpenCurrentDatabase(DBName)
    db = oAccess.CurrentDB()
```

```
rs = db.OpenRecordset(TBLName)
```

Attribute XML

TEXT EXAMPLE

```
ws  = Win32com.client.Dispatch("WScript.Shell")
   fso  = Win32com.client.Dispatch("Scripting.FileSystemObject")
   txtstream  = fso.OpenTextFile("C:\Products.xml", 2, True, -2)
   txtstream.WriteLine("<?xml  version='1.0'  encoding='iso-8859-
1'?>")
   txtstream.WriteLine("<data>")
   rs.MoveFirst()
   While rs.EOF = false:
     txtstream.WriteLine("<Products>")
     For x in range(rs.Fields.Count):
       txtstream.WriteLine("<property     name    =    """    +
rs.Fields[x].Name + """" value=""""" + rs.Fields[x].value + """"/>")

     txtstream.WriteLine("</Products>")
   rs.MoveNext()

   txtstream.WriteLine("</data>")
   txtstream.Close
```

```
xmldoc  = win32com.client.Dispatch("MSXML2.DOMDocument")
pi  =  xmldoc.CreateProcessingInstruction("xml",  "version='1.0'
encoding='ISO-8859-1'")
oRoot = xmldoc.CreateElement("data")
xmldoc.AppendChild(pi)
rs.MoveFirst()
While rs.EOF = false:
  oNode = xmldoc.CreateNode(1, \"" + TBLName + "\", "")
  For x in range(rs.Fields.Count):
    oNode1 = xmldoc.CreateNode(1, "Property", "")
    oAtt = xmldoc.CreateAttribute("NAME")
    oAtt.Value = rs.Fields[x].Name
    oNode1.Attributes.SetNamedItem(oAtt)
    oAtt = xmldoc.CreateAttribute("DATATYPE")
    oAtt.Value = str(rs.Fields[x].Type)
    oNode1.Attributes.SetNamedItem(oAtt)
    oAtt = xmldoc.CreateAttribute("SIZE")
    oAtt.Value = len(str(rs.Fields[x].Value))
    oNode1.Attributes.SetNamedItem(oAtt)
    oAtt = xmldoc.CreateAttribute("Value")
    oAtt.Value = str(rs.Fields[x].Value)
    oNode1.Attributes.SetNamedItem(oAtt)
    oNode.AppendChild(oNode1)

  oRoot.AppendChild(oNode)
  rs.MoveNext()

xmldoc.AppendChild(oRoot)
```

```
ws = win32com.client.Dispatch("WScript.Shell")
xmldoc.Save(ws.CurrentDirectory + "\\" + TBLName + ".xml")
```

Element XML

TEXT EXAMPLE

```
ws = Win32com.client.Dispatch("WScript.Shell")
txtstream          =          fso.OpenTextFile(ws.CurrentDirectory          +
"\Products.xml", 2, true, -2)
txtstream.WriteLine("<?xml version='1.0' encoding='iso-8859-
1'?>")
txtstream.WriteLine("<data>")
rs.MoveFirst()
While rs.EOF = false:
    txtstream.WriteLine("<products>")
    For x in range(rs.Fields.Count):
        txtstream.WriteLine("<" + rs.Fields[x].Name + ">" +
rs.Fields[x].value +"</" + rs.Fields[x].Name + ">")

    txtstream.WriteLine("</products>")
    rs.MoveNext()

txtstream.WriteLine("</data>")
txtstream.close
```

USING THE DOM

```
xmldoc = win32com.client.Dispatch("MSXML2.DOMDocument")
pi = xmldoc.CreateProcessingInstruction("xml", "version='1.0'
encoding='ISO-8859-1'")
oRoot = xmldoc.CreateElement("data")
xmldoc.AppendChild(pi)
rs.MoveFirst()
While rs.EOF = false:
  oNode = xmldoc.CreateNode(1, \"" + TBLName + "\", "")
  For x in range(rs.Fields.Count):
    oNode1 = xmldoc.CreateNode(1, \"" + rs.Fields[x].Name + "\",
"")
    oNode1.Text = str(rs.Fields[x].Value)
    oNode.AppendChild(oNode1)

  oRoot.AppendChild(oNode)
  rs.MoveNext()

xmldoc.AppendChild(oRoot)
ws = win32com.client.Dispatch("WScript.Shell")
xmldoc.Save(ws.CurrentDirectory + "\\" + TBLName + ".xml")
```

Element XML For XSL

....

TEXT EXAMPLE

```
ws = Win32com.client.Dispatch("WScript.Shell")
txtstream = fso.OpenTextFile(ws.CurrentDirectory +
"\Products.xml", 2, true, -2)
```

```
txtstream.WriteLine("<?xml version='1.0' encoding='iso-8859-
1'?>")
txtstream.WriteLine("<?xml-stylesheet          type='Text/xsl'
href=""""" + ws.CurrentDirectory + "\Products.xml.xsl"""?>")
txtstream.WriteLine("<data>")
rs.MoveFirst()
While rs.EOF = false:
    txtstream.WriteLine("<products>")
    For x in range(rs.Fields.Count):
        txtstream.WriteLine("<" + rs.Fields[x].Name + ">" +
rs.Fields[x].value +"</" + rs.Fields[x].Name + ">")

    txtstream.WriteLine("</products>")
    rs.MoveNext()

txtstream.WriteLine("</data>")
txtstream.close
```

USING THE DOM

```
xmldoc = win32com.client.Dispatch("MSXML2.DOMDocument")
pi = xmldoc.CreateProcessingInstruction("xml", "version='1.0'
encoding='ISO-8859-1'")
```

```
pii       =       xmldoc.CreateProcessingInstruction("xml-stylesheet",
"type='text/xsl' href='Process.xsl'")
oRoot = xmldoc.CreateElement("data")
xmldoc.AppendChild(pi)
xmldoc.AppendChild(pii)

rs.MoveFirst()
While rs.EOF = false:
  oNode = xmldoc.CreateNode(1, \"" + TBLName + "\", "")
  For x in range(rs.Fields.Count):
    oNode1 = xmldoc.CreateNode(1, \"" +  rs.Fields[x].Name + "\",
"")
    oNode1.Text = str(rs.Fields[x].Value)
    oNode.AppendChild(oNode1)

  oRoot.AppendChild(oNode)
  rs.MoveNext()

xmldoc.AppendChild(oRoot)
ws = win32com.client.Dispatch("WScript.Shell")
xmldoc.Save(ws.CurrentDirectory + "\\" + TBLName + ".xml")
```

Schema XML

TEXT EXAMPLE

```
ws  = Win32com.client.Dispatch("WScript.Shell")
txtstream  = fso.OpenTextFile(ws.CurrentDirectory +
"\Products.xml", 2, true, -2)
txtstream.WriteLine("<?xml version='1.0' encoding='iso-8859-
1'?>")
txtstream.WriteLine("<data>")
rs.MoveFirst()
While rs.EOF = false:
   txtstream.WriteLine("<products>")
   For x in range(rs.Fields.Count):
      txtstream.WriteLine("<" + rs.Fields[x].Name + ">" +
rs.Fields[x].value +"</" + rs.Fields[x].Name + ">")

      txtstream.WriteLine("</products>")
      rs.MoveNext()

txtstream.WriteLine("</data>")
txtstream.close

rs1 = win32com.client.Dispatch("ADODB.Recordset")
rs1.ActiveConnection          =          "Provider=MSDAOSP;Data
Source=MSXML2.DSOControl;"
rs1.CursorLocation = 3
rs1.LockType = 3
rs1.Open(ws.CurrentDirectory + "\\" + TBLName + "E.xml")
fso = win32com.client.Dispatch("Scripting.FileSystemObject")
if fso.FileExists(ws.CurrentDirectory + "\\" + TBLName + "S.xml")
== True:
   fso.DeleteFile(ws.CurrentDirectory + "\\" + TBLName + "S.xml")

rs.Save(ws.CurrentDirectory + "\\ProcessS.xml", 1)
```

USING THE DOM

```
xmldoc = win32com.client.Dispatch("MSXML2.DOMDocument")
pi   =   xmldoc.CreateProcessingInstruction("xml",   "version='1.0'
encoding='ISO-8859-1'")
oRoot = xmldoc.CreateElement("data")
xmldoc.AppendChild(pi)
rs.MoveFirst()
while rs.EOF = false:
   oNode = xmldoc.CreateNode(1, \"" + TBLName + "\", "")
   for x in range(rs.Fields.Count):
      oNode1 = xmldoc.CreateNode(1, \"" +  rs.Fields[x].Name + "\",
"")
      oNode1.Text = str(rs.Fields[x].Value)
      oNode.AppendChild(oNode1)

   oRoot.AppendChild(oNode)
   rs.MoveNext()

xmldoc.AppendChild(oRoot)
ws = win32com.client.Dispatch("WScript.Shell")
xmldoc.Save(ws.CurrentDirectory + "\\" + TBLName + ".xml")
xmldoc = None

rs1 = win32com.client.Dispatch("ADODB.Recordset")
rs1.ActiveConnection            =            "Provider=MSDAOSP;Data
Source=MSXML2.DSOControl;"
rs1.CursorLocation = 3
rs1.LockType = 3
```

```
rs1.Open(ws.CurrentDirectory + "\\" + TBLName + "E.xml")
fso = win32com.client.Dispatch("Scripting.FileSystemObject")
if fso.FileExists(ws.CurrentDirectory + "\\" + TBLName + "S.xml")
== True:
    fso.DeleteFile(ws.CurrentDirectory + "\\" + TBLName + "S.xml")

rs.Save(ws.CurrentDirectory + "\\ProcessS.xml", 1)
```

CREATING XSL FILES FROM ACCESS

Rendering your XML Files in Style

Nothing is prettier than a quality XSL stylesheet.
—R. T. Edwards

T here is nothing great about xml when you're just looking at an xml file. But as soon as you add an HTML based XSL file to render it, suddenly, it looks professional and understandable.

There four ways to use XSL, Single Line Horizontal, Multi line Horizontal, Single Line Vertical and Multi line Vertical.

Single Line Horizontal Example

```
import win32com.client
import string

oAccess = win32com.client.Dispatch("Access.Application")
oAccess.OpenCurrentDatabase(DBName)
db = oAccess.CurrentDB()
rs = db.OpenRecordset(TBLName)
```

```
txtstream=          fso.OpenTextfile(ws.CurrentDirectory          +
"\\Process.xsl", 2, True, -2)
    txtstream.WriteLine("<?xml  version='1.0'  encoding='iso-8859-
1'?>")
    txtstream.WriteLine("<xsl:stylesheet            version=\"1.0\"
xmlns:xsl=\"http://www.w3.org/1999/XSL/Transform\">")
    txtstream.WriteLine("<xsl:template match=\"/\">")
    txtstream.WriteLine("<html>")
    txtstream.WriteLine("<head>")
    txtstream.WriteLine("<title>Process</title>")
    txtstream.WriteLine("</head>")
    txtstream.WriteLine("<body>")
    txtstream.WriteLine("<table Width ='100%'>")
    txtstream.WriteLine("<tr>")
    for x in range(rs.Fields.Count):
        txtstream.WriteLine("<th   align='left'   nowrap='true'>"   +
rs.Fields[x].Name + "</th>")

    txtstream.WriteLine("</tr>")
    txtstream.WriteLine("<tr>")
    for x in range(rs.Fields.Count):
        txtstream.WriteLine("<td                        align='left'
nowrap='true'><xsl:value-of select=\"data/" + TBLName + "/" +
rs.Fields[x].Name + "\"/></td>")

    txtstream.WriteLine("</tr>")
    txtstream.WriteLine("</table>")
    txtstream.WriteLine("</body>")
    txtstream.WriteLine("</html>")
    txtstream.WriteLine("</xsl:template>")
```

```
txtstream.WriteLine("</xsl:stylesheet>")
txtstream.Close()
```

Multi Line Horizontal

```
import win32com.client
import string

oAccess = win32com.client.Dispatch("Access.Application")
oAccess.OpenCurrentDatabase(DBName)
db = oAccess.CurrentDB()
rs = db.OpenRecordset(TBLName)

ws = win32com.client.Dispatch("WScript.Shell")
fso = win32com.client.Dispatch("Scripting.FileSystemObject")
txtstream=        fso.OpenTextfile(ws.CurrentDirectory        +
"\\Process.xsl", 2, True, -2)
txtstream.WriteLine("<?xml version='1.0' encoding='iso-8859-
1'?>")
txtstream.WriteLine("<xsl:stylesheet              version=\"1.0\"
xmlns:xsl=\"http://www.w3.org/1999/XSL/Transform\">")
txtstream.WriteLine("<xsl:template match=\"/\">")
txtstream.WriteLine("<html>")
txtstream.WriteLine("<head>")
txtstream.WriteLine("<title>Process</title>")
txtstream.WriteLine("</head>")
txtstream.WriteLine("<body>")
txtstream.WriteLine("<table Width ='100%'>")
txtstream.WriteLine("<tr>")
 for x in range(rs.Fields.Count):
```

```python
        txtstream.WriteLine("<th  align='left'  nowrap='true'>"  +
rs.Fields[x].Name + "</th>")

    txtstream.WriteLine("</tr>")
    txtstream.WriteLine("<xsl:for-each select=\"data\" + TBLName
+ "\">")
    txtstream.WriteLine("<tr>")
     for x in range(rs.Fields.Count):
        txtstream.WriteLine("<td                        align='left'
nowrap='true'><xsl:value-of   select=\""   +   rs.Fields[x].Name   +
"\"/></td>")

    txtstream.WriteLine("</tr>")
    txtstream.WriteLine("</xsl:for-each>")
    txtstream.WriteLine("</table>")
    txtstream.WriteLine("</body>")
    txtstream.WriteLine("</html>")
    txtstream.WriteLine("</xsl:template>")
    txtstream.WriteLine("</xsl:stylesheet>")
    txtstream.Close()
```

Single Line Vertical

```python
  import win32com.client
  import string

  oAccess = win32com.client.Dispatch("Access.Application")
  oAccess.OpenCurrentDatabase(DBName)
  db = oAccess.CurrentDB()
  rs = db.OpenRecordset(TBLName)
```

```
ws = win32com.client.Dispatch("WScript.Shell")
fso = win32com.client.Dispatch("Scripting.FileSystemObject")
txtstream=        fso.OpenTextfile(ws.CurrentDirectory        +
"\\Process.xsl", 2, True, -2)
txtstream.WriteLine("<?xml version='1.0' encoding='iso-8859-
1'?>")
txtstream.WriteLine("<xsl:stylesheet               version=\"1.0\"
xmlns:xsl=\"http://www.w3.org/1999/XSL/Transform\">")
txtstream.WriteLine("<xsl:template match=\"/\">")
txtstream.WriteLine("<html>")
txtstream.WriteLine("<head>")
txtstream.WriteLine("<title>Process</title>")
txtstream.WriteLine("</head>")
txtstream.WriteLine("<body>")
txtstream.WriteLine("<table Width ='100%'>")
 for x in range(rs.Fields.Count):
    txtstream.WriteLine("<tr><th align='left' nowrap='true'>" +
rs.Fields[x].Name        +        "</th><td        align='left'
nowrap='true'><xsl:value-of select=\"data/" + TBLName + "/" +
rs.Fields[x].Name + "\"/></td></tr>")

txtstream.WriteLine("</table>")
txtstream.WriteLine("</body>")
txtstream.WriteLine("</html>")
txtstream.WriteLine("</xsl:template>")
txtstream.WriteLine("</xsl:stylesheet>")
txtstream.Close()
```

Multi Line Vertical

```
import win32com.client
import string

oAccess = win32com.client.Dispatch("Access.Application")
oAccess.OpenCurrentDatabase(DBName)
db = oAccess.CurrentDB()
rs = db.OpenRecordset(TBLName)

txtstream= fso.OpenTextfile(ws.CurrentDirectory +
"\\Process.xsl", 2, True, -2)
txtstream.WriteLine("<?xml version='1.0' encoding='iso-8859-
1'?>")
txtstream.WriteLine("<xsl:stylesheet version=\"1.0\"
xmlns:xsl=\"http://www.w3.org/1999/XSL/Transform\">")
txtstream.WriteLine("<xsl:template match=\"/\">")
txtstream.WriteLine("<html>")
txtstream.WriteLine("<head>")
txtstream.WriteLine("<title>Process</title>")
txtstream.WriteLine("</head>")
txtstream.WriteLine("<body>")
txtstream.WriteLine("<table Width ='100%'>")
for x in range(rs.Fields.Count):
    txtstream.WriteLine("<tr><th align='left' nowrap='true'>" +
rs.Fields[x].Name + "</th><xsl:for-each select=\"data\" +
TBLName + "\"><td align='left' nowrap='true'><xsl:value-of
select=\"" + rs.Fields[x].Name + "\"/></td></xsl:for-each></tr>")

txtstream.WriteLine("</table>")
txtstream.WriteLine("</body>")
txtstream.WriteLine("</html>")
```

```
txtstream.WriteLine("</xsl:template>")
txtstream.WriteLine("</xsl:stylesheet>")
txtstream.Close()
```

STYLESHEETS

Do you proud every time

Stylesheets aren't just to make a page look remarkable, they also make you look remarkable, too.
— R. T. Edwards

hat is the first thing you see when you go to a website and look at
W the home page for the first time? It is the level of professionalism
– that keen insight to attention to details – that draws you in.
Speaks to you. Tells you that the site wants you to stay a while and
shares with you a common ground.

The unseen hero – css. I've created some stylesheets—listed
below—so you can try and use with the various web related
programs.

NONE

```
txtstream.WriteLine("<style type='text/css'>")
txtstream.WriteLine("th")
txtstream.WriteLine("")
```

```
txtstream.WriteLine("   COLOR: white;")
txtstream.WriteLine(" Next")
txtstream.WriteLine("td")
txtstream.WriteLine(""")
txtstream.WriteLine("   COLOR: white;")
txtstream.WriteLine(" Next")
txtstream.WriteLine("</style>")
```

BLACK AND WHITE TEXT

```
txtstream.WriteLine("<style type='text/css'>")
txtstream.WriteLine("th")
txtstream.WriteLine(""")
txtstream.WriteLine("   COLOR: white;")
txtstream.WriteLine("   BACKGROUND-COLOR: black;")
txtstream.WriteLine("     FONT-FAMILY:font-family: Cambria, serif;")
txtstream.WriteLine("   FONT-SIZE: 12px;")
txtstream.WriteLine("   text-align: left;")
txtstream.WriteLine("   white-Space: nowrap;")
txtstream.WriteLine(" Next")
txtstream.WriteLine("td")
txtstream.WriteLine(""")
txtstream.WriteLine("   COLOR: white;")
txtstream.WriteLine("   BACKGROUND-COLOR: black;")
txtstream.WriteLine("     FONT-FAMILY: font-family: Cambria, serif;")
txtstream.WriteLine("   FONT-SIZE: 12px;")
txtstream.WriteLine("   text-align: left;")
txtstream.WriteLine("   white-Space: nowrap;")
txtstream.WriteLine(" Next")
txtstream.WriteLine("div")
```

```
txtstream.WriteLine("")
txtstream.WriteLine("   COLOR: white;")
txtstream.WriteLine("   BACKGROUND-COLOR: black;")
txtstream.WriteLine("    FONT-FAMILY: font-family: Cambria,
serif;")
txtstream.WriteLine("   FONT-SIZE: 10px;")
txtstream.WriteLine("   text-align: left;")
txtstream.WriteLine("   white-Space: nowrap;")
txtstream.WriteLine(" Next")
txtstream.WriteLine("span")
txtstream.WriteLine("")
txtstream.WriteLine("   COLOR: white;")
txtstream.WriteLine("   BACKGROUND-COLOR: black;")
txtstream.WriteLine("    FONT-FAMILY: font-family: Cambria,
serif;")
txtstream.WriteLine("   FONT-SIZE: 10px;")
txtstream.WriteLine("   text-align: left;")
txtstream.WriteLine("   white-Space: nowrap;")
txtstream.WriteLine("   display:inline-block;")
txtstream.WriteLine("   width: 100%;")
txtstream.WriteLine(" Next")
txtstream.WriteLine("textarea")
txtstream.WriteLine("")
txtstream.WriteLine("   COLOR: white;")
txtstream.WriteLine("   BACKGROUND-COLOR: black;")
txtstream.WriteLine("    FONT-FAMILY: font-family: Cambria,
serif;")
txtstream.WriteLine("   FONT-SIZE: 10px;")
txtstream.WriteLine("   text-align: left;")
txtstream.WriteLine("   white-Space: nowrap;")
txtstream.WriteLine("   width: 100%;")
txtstream.WriteLine(" Next")
```

```
txtstream.WriteLine("select")
txtstream.WriteLine("“)
txtstream.WriteLine("   COLOR: white;")
txtstream.WriteLine("   BACKGROUND-COLOR: black;")
txtstream.WriteLine("    FONT-FAMILY: font-family: Cambria, serif;")
txtstream.WriteLine("   FONT-SIZE: 10px;")
txtstream.WriteLine("   text-align: left;")
txtstream.WriteLine("   white-Space: nowrap;")
txtstream.WriteLine("   width: 100%;")
txtstream.WriteLine(" Next")
txtstream.WriteLine("input")
txtstream.WriteLine("“)
txtstream.WriteLine("   COLOR: white;")
txtstream.WriteLine("   BACKGROUND-COLOR: black;")
txtstream.WriteLine("    FONT-FAMILY: font-family: Cambria, serif;")
txtstream.WriteLine("   FONT-SIZE: 12px;")
txtstream.WriteLine("   text-align: left;")
txtstream.WriteLine("   display:table-cell;")
txtstream.WriteLine("   white-Space: nowrap;")
txtstream.WriteLine(" Next")
txtstream.WriteLine("h1 “)
txtstream.WriteLine("color: antiquewhite;")
txtstream.WriteLine("text-shadow: 1px 1px 1px black;")
txtstream.WriteLine("padding: 3px;")
txtstream.WriteLine("text-align: center;")
txtstream.WriteLine("box-shadow:  inSet  2px  2px  5px rgba(0,0,0,0.5), inSet -2px -2px 5px rgba(255,255,255,0.5);")
txtstream.WriteLine(" Next")
txtstream.WriteLine("</style>“)
```

COLORED TEXT

```
txtstream.WriteLine("<style type='text/css'>")
txtstream.WriteLine("th")
txtstream.WriteLine("")
txtstream.WriteLine("   COLOR: darkred;")
txtstream.WriteLine("   BACKGROUND-COLOR: #eeeeee;")
txtstream.WriteLine("    FONT-FAMILY:font-family: Cambria,
serif;")
txtstream.WriteLine("   FONT-SIZE: 12px;")
txtstream.WriteLine("   text-align: left;")
txtstream.WriteLine("   white-Space: nowrap;")
txtstream.WriteLine(" }")
txtstream.WriteLine("td")
txtstream.WriteLine("")
txtstream.WriteLine("   COLOR: navy;")
txtstream.WriteLine("   BACKGROUND-COLOR: #eeeeee;")
txtstream.WriteLine("    FONT-FAMILY: font-family: Cambria,
serif;")
txtstream.WriteLine("   FONT-SIZE: 12px;")
txtstream.WriteLine("   text-align: left;")
txtstream.WriteLine("   white-Space: nowrap;")
txtstream.WriteLine(" }")
txtstream.WriteLine("div")
txtstream.WriteLine("")
txtstream.WriteLine("   COLOR: white;")
txtstream.WriteLine("   BACKGROUND-COLOR: navy;")
txtstream.WriteLine("    FONT-FAMILY: font-family: Cambria,
serif;")
txtstream.WriteLine("   FONT-SIZE: 10px;")
txtstream.WriteLine("   text-align: left;")
txtstream.WriteLine("   white-Space: nowrap;")
```

```
txtstream.WriteLine(" }")
txtstream.WriteLine("span")
txtstream.WriteLine("")
txtstream.WriteLine("    COLOR: white;")
txtstream.WriteLine("    BACKGROUND-COLOR: navy;")
txtstream.WriteLine("     FONT-FAMILY: font-family: Cambria,
serif;")
txtstream.WriteLine("    FONT-SIZE: 10px;")
txtstream.WriteLine("    text-align: left;")
txtstream.WriteLine("    white-Space: nowrap;")
txtstream.WriteLine("    display:inline-block;")
txtstream.WriteLine("    width: 100%;")
txtstream.WriteLine(" }")
txtstream.WriteLine("textarea")
txtstream.WriteLine("")
txtstream.WriteLine("    COLOR: white;")
txtstream.WriteLine("    BACKGROUND-COLOR: navy;")
txtstream.WriteLine("     FONT-FAMILY: font-family: Cambria,
serif;")
txtstream.WriteLine("    FONT-SIZE: 10px;")
txtstream.WriteLine("    text-align: left;")
txtstream.WriteLine("    white-Space: nowrap;")
txtstream.WriteLine("    width: 100%;")
txtstream.WriteLine(" }")
txtstream.WriteLine("select")
txtstream.WriteLine("")
txtstream.WriteLine("    COLOR: white;")
txtstream.WriteLine("    BACKGROUND-COLOR: navy;")
txtstream.WriteLine("     FONT-FAMILY: font-family: Cambria,
serif;")
txtstream.WriteLine("    FONT-SIZE: 10px;")
txtstream.WriteLine("    text-align: left;")
```

```
txtstream.WriteLine("    white-Space: nowrap;")
txtstream.WriteLine("    width: 100%;")
txtstream.WriteLine(" }")
txtstream.WriteLine("input")
txtstream.WriteLine("")
txtstream.WriteLine("    COLOR: white;")
txtstream.WriteLine("    BACKGROUND-COLOR: navy;")
txtstream.WriteLine("    FONT-FAMILY: font-family: Cambria, serif;")
txtstream.WriteLine("    FONT-SIZE: 12px;")
txtstream.WriteLine("    text-align: left;")
txtstream.WriteLine("    display:table-cell;")
txtstream.WriteLine("    white-Space: nowrap;")
txtstream.WriteLine(" }")
txtstream.WriteLine("h1 ")
txtstream.WriteLine("color: antiquewhite;")
txtstream.WriteLine("text-shadow: 1px 1px 1px black;")
txtstream.WriteLine("padding: 3px;")
txtstream.WriteLine("text-align: center;")
txtstream.WriteLine("box-shadow:    inSet    2px    2px    5px rgba(0,0,0,0.5), inSet -2px -2px 5px rgba(255,255,255,0.5);")
txtstream.WriteLine(" }")
txtstream.WriteLine("</style>")
```

OSCILLATING ROW COLORS

```
txtstream.WriteLine("<style>")
txtstream.WriteLine("th")
txtstream.WriteLine("")
txtstream.WriteLine("    COLOR: white;")
```

```
txtstream.WriteLine(" BACKGROUND-COLOR: navy;")
txtstream.WriteLine("  FONT-FAMILY:font-family: Cambria,
serif;")
txtstream.WriteLine(" FONT-SIZE: 12px;")
txtstream.WriteLine(" text-align: left;")
txtstream.WriteLine(" white-Space: nowrap;")
txtstream.WriteLine(" }")
txtstream.WriteLine("td")
txtstream.WriteLine("")
txtstream.WriteLine(" COLOR: navy;")
txtstream.WriteLine("  FONT-FAMILY: font-family: Cambria,
serif;")
txtstream.WriteLine(" FONT-SIZE: 12px;")
txtstream.WriteLine(" text-align: left;")
txtstream.WriteLine(" white-Space: nowrap;")
txtstream.WriteLine(" }")
txtstream.WriteLine("div")
txtstream.WriteLine("")
txtstream.WriteLine(" COLOR: navy;")
txtstream.WriteLine("  FONT-FAMILY: font-family: Cambria,
serif;")
txtstream.WriteLine(" FONT-SIZE: 12px;")
txtstream.WriteLine(" text-align: left;")
txtstream.WriteLine(" white-Space: nowrap;")
txtstream.WriteLine(" }")
txtstream.WriteLine("span")
txtstream.WriteLine("")
txtstream.WriteLine(" COLOR: navy;")
txtstream.WriteLine("  FONT-FAMILY: font-family: Cambria,
serif;")
txtstream.WriteLine(" FONT-SIZE: 12px;")
txtstream.WriteLine(" text-align: left;")
```

```
txtstream.WriteLine("   white-Space: nowrap;")
txtstream.WriteLine("   width: 100%;")
txtstream.WriteLine(" }")
txtstream.WriteLine("textarea")
txtstream.WriteLine("")
txtstream.WriteLine("   COLOR: navy;")
txtstream.WriteLine("    FONT-FAMILY: font-family: Cambria,
serif;")
txtstream.WriteLine("   FONT-SIZE: 12px;")
txtstream.WriteLine("   text-align: left;")
txtstream.WriteLine("   white-Space: nowrap;")
txtstream.WriteLine("   display:inline-block;")
txtstream.WriteLine("   width: 100%;")
txtstream.WriteLine(" }")
txtstream.WriteLine("select")
txtstream.WriteLine("")
txtstream.WriteLine("   COLOR: navy;")
txtstream.WriteLine("    FONT-FAMILY: font-family: Cambria,
serif;")
txtstream.WriteLine("   FONT-SIZE: 10px;")
txtstream.WriteLine("   text-align: left;")
txtstream.WriteLine("   white-Space: nowrap;")
txtstream.WriteLine("   display:inline-block;")
txtstream.WriteLine("   width: 100%;")
txtstream.WriteLine(" }")
txtstream.WriteLine("input")
txtstream.WriteLine("")
txtstream.WriteLine("   COLOR: navy;")
txtstream.WriteLine("    FONT-FAMILY: font-family: Cambria,
serif;")
txtstream.WriteLine("   FONT-SIZE: 12px;")
txtstream.WriteLine("   text-align: left;")
```

txtstream.WriteLine("   display:table-cell;")

txtstream.WriteLine("   white-Space: nowrap;")

txtstream.WriteLine(" }")

txtstream.WriteLine("h1 ")

txtstream.WriteLine("color: antiquewhite;")

txtstream.WriteLine("text-shadow: 1px 1px 1px black;")

txtstream.WriteLine("padding: 3px;")

txtstream.WriteLine("text-align: center;")

txtstream.WriteLine("box-shadow: inSet   2px   2px   5px rgba(0,0,0,0.5), inSet -2px -2px 5px rgba(255,255,255,0.5);")

txtstream.WriteLine(" }")

txtstream.WriteLine("tr:nth-child(even)background-color:#f2f2f2; }")

txtstream.WriteLine("tr:nth-child(odd)background-color:#cccccc; color:#f2f2f2; }")

txtstream.WriteLine("</style>")

GHOST DECORATED

txtstream.WriteLine("<style type='text/css'>")

txtstream.WriteLine("th")

txtstream.WriteLine("")

txtstream.WriteLine("   COLOR: black;")

txtstream.WriteLine("   BACKGROUND-COLOR: white;")

txtstream.WriteLine("   FONT-FAMILY:font-family: Cambria, serif;")

txtstream.WriteLine("   FONT-SIZE: 12px;")

txtstream.WriteLine("   text-align: left;")

txtstream.WriteLine("   white-Space: nowrap;")

txtstream.WriteLine(" }")

txtstream.WriteLine("td")

txtstream.WriteLine("")

```
txtstream.WriteLine("   COLOR: black;")
txtstream.WriteLine("   BACKGROUND-COLOR: white;")
txtstream.WriteLine("    FONT-FAMILY: font-family: Cambria,
serif;")
txtstream.WriteLine("   FONT-SIZE: 12px;")
txtstream.WriteLine("   text-align: left;")
txtstream.WriteLine("   white-Space: nowrap;")
txtstream.WriteLine(" }")
txtstream.WriteLine("div")
txtstream.WriteLine("")
txtstream.WriteLine("   COLOR: black;")
txtstream.WriteLine("   BACKGROUND-COLOR: white;")
txtstream.WriteLine("    FONT-FAMILY: font-family: Cambria,
serif;")
txtstream.WriteLine("   FONT-SIZE: 10px;")
txtstream.WriteLine("   text-align: left;")
txtstream.WriteLine("   white-Space: nowrap;")
txtstream.WriteLine(" }")
txtstream.WriteLine("span")
txtstream.WriteLine("")
txtstream.WriteLine("   COLOR: black;")
txtstream.WriteLine("   BACKGROUND-COLOR: white;")
txtstream.WriteLine("    FONT-FAMILY: font-family: Cambria,
serif;")
txtstream.WriteLine("   FONT-SIZE: 10px;")
txtstream.WriteLine("   text-align: left;")
txtstream.WriteLine("   white-Space: nowrap;")
txtstream.WriteLine("   display:inline-block;")
txtstream.WriteLine("   width: 100%;")
txtstream.WriteLine(" }")
txtstream.WriteLine("textarea")
txtstream.WriteLine("")
```

```
txtstream.WriteLine("    COLOR: black;")
txtstream.WriteLine("    BACKGROUND-COLOR: white;")
txtstream.WriteLine("      FONT-FAMILY: font-family: Cambria,
serif;")
txtstream.WriteLine("    FONT-SIZE: 10px;")
txtstream.WriteLine("    text-align: left;")
txtstream.WriteLine("    white-Space: nowrap;")
txtstream.WriteLine("    width: 100%;")
txtstream.WriteLine(" }")
txtstream.WriteLine("select")
txtstream.WriteLine("")
txtstream.WriteLine("    COLOR: black;")
txtstream.WriteLine("    BACKGROUND-COLOR: white;")
txtstream.WriteLine("      FONT-FAMILY: font-family: Cambria,
serif;")
txtstream.WriteLine("    FONT-SIZE: 10px;")
txtstream.WriteLine("    text-align: left;")
txtstream.WriteLine("    white-Space: nowrap;")
txtstream.WriteLine("    width: 100%;")
txtstream.WriteLine(" }")
txtstream.WriteLine("input")
txtstream.WriteLine("")
txtstream.WriteLine("    COLOR: black;")
txtstream.WriteLine("    BACKGROUND-COLOR: white;")
txtstream.WriteLine("      FONT-FAMILY: font-family: Cambria,
serif;")
txtstream.WriteLine("    FONT-SIZE: 12px;")
txtstream.WriteLine("    text-align: left;")
txtstream.WriteLine("    display:table-cell;")
txtstream.WriteLine("    white-Space: nowrap;")
txtstream.WriteLine(" }")
txtstream.WriteLine("h1 ")
```

```
txtstream.WriteLine("color: antiquewhite;")
txtstream.WriteLine("text-shadow: 1px 1px 1px black;")
txtstream.WriteLine("padding: 3px;")
txtstream.WriteLine("text-align: center;")
txtstream.WriteLine("box-shadow:     inSet     2px     2px     5px
rgba(0,0,0,0.5), inSet -2px -2px 5px rgba(255,255,255,0.5);")
txtstream.WriteLine(" }")
txtstream.WriteLine("</style>")
```

3D


```
txtstream.WriteLine("<style type='text/css'>")
txtstream.WriteLine("body")
txtstream.WriteLine("")
txtstream.WriteLine("    PADDING-RIGHT: 0px;")
txtstream.WriteLine("    PADDING-LEFT: 0px;")
txtstream.WriteLine("    PADDING-BOTTOM: 0px;")
txtstream.WriteLine("    MARGIN: 0px;")
txtstream.WriteLine("    COLOR: #333;")
txtstream.WriteLine("    PADDING-TOP: 0px;")
txtstream.WriteLine("          FONT-FAMILY:  verdana,  arial,
helvetica, sans-serif;")
txtstream.WriteLine(" }")
txtstream.WriteLine("table")
txtstream.WriteLine("")
txtstream.WriteLine("    BORDER-RIGHT: #999999 3px solid;")
txtstream.WriteLine("    PADDING-RIGHT: 6px;")
txtstream.WriteLine("    PADDING-LEFT: 6px;")
txtstream.WriteLine("    FONT-WEIGHT: Bold;")
txtstream.WriteLine("    FONT-SIZE: 14px;")
txtstream.WriteLine("    PADDING-BOTTOM: 6px;")
```

```
txtstream.WriteLine("    COLOR: Peru;")
txtstream.WriteLine("    LINE-HEIGHT: 14px;")
txtstream.WriteLine("    PADDING-TOP: 6px;")
txtstream.WriteLine("    BORDER-BOTTOM: #999 1px solid;")
txtstream.WriteLine("    BACKGROUND-COLOR: #eeeeee;")
txtstream.WriteLine("        FONT-FAMILY: verdana, arial, helvetica, sans-serif;")
txtstream.WriteLine("    FONT-SIZE: 12px;")
txtstream.WriteLine(" }")
txtstream.WriteLine("th")
txtstream.WriteLine("“)
txtstream.WriteLine("    BORDER-RIGHT: #999999 3px solid;")
txtstream.WriteLine("    PADDING-RIGHT: 6px;")
txtstream.WriteLine("    PADDING-LEFT: 6px;")
txtstream.WriteLine("    FONT-WEIGHT: Bold;")
txtstream.WriteLine("    FONT-SIZE: 14px;")
txtstream.WriteLine("    PADDING-BOTTOM: 6px;")
txtstream.WriteLine("    COLOR: darkred;")
txtstream.WriteLine("    LINE-HEIGHT: 14px;")
txtstream.WriteLine("    PADDING-TOP: 6px;")
txtstream.WriteLine("    BORDER-BOTTOM: #999 1px solid;")
txtstream.WriteLine("    BACKGROUND-COLOR: #eeeeee;")
txtstream.WriteLine("        FONT-FAMILY:font-family: Cambria, serif;")
txtstream.WriteLine("    FONT-SIZE: 12px;")
txtstream.WriteLine("    text-align: left;")
txtstream.WriteLine("    white-Space: nowrap;")
txtstream.WriteLine(" }")
txtstream.WriteLine(".th")
txtstream.WriteLine("“)
txtstream.WriteLine("    BORDER-RIGHT: #999999 2px solid;")
txtstream.WriteLine("    PADDING-RIGHT: 6px;")
```

```
txtstream.WriteLine("    PADDING-LEFT: 6px;")
txtstream.WriteLine("    FONT-WEIGHT: Bold;")
txtstream.WriteLine("    PADDING-BOTTOM: 6px;")
txtstream.WriteLine("    COLOR: black;")
txtstream.WriteLine("    PADDING-TOP: 6px;")
txtstream.WriteLine("    BORDER-BOTTOM: #999 2px solid;")
txtstream.WriteLine("    BACKGROUND-COLOR: #eeeeee;")
txtstream.WriteLine("     FONT-FAMILY: font-family: Cambria, serif;")
txtstream.WriteLine("    FONT-SIZE: 10px;")
txtstream.WriteLine("    text-align: right;")
txtstream.WriteLine("    white-Space: nowrap;")
txtstream.WriteLine(" }")
txtstream.WriteLine("td")
txtstream.WriteLine("")
txtstream.WriteLine("    BORDER-RIGHT: #999999 3px solid;")
txtstream.WriteLine("    PADDING-RIGHT: 6px;")
txtstream.WriteLine("    PADDING-LEFT: 6px;")
txtstream.WriteLine("    FONT-WEIGHT: Normal;")
txtstream.WriteLine("    PADDING-BOTTOM: 6px;")
txtstream.WriteLine("    COLOR: navy;")
txtstream.WriteLine("    LINE-HEIGHT: 14px;")
txtstream.WriteLine("    PADDING-TOP: 6px;")
txtstream.WriteLine("    BORDER-BOTTOM: #999 1px solid;")
txtstream.WriteLine("    BACKGROUND-COLOR: #eeeeee;")
txtstream.WriteLine("     FONT-FAMILY: font-family: Cambria, serif;")
txtstream.WriteLine("    FONT-SIZE: 12px;")
txtstream.WriteLine("    text-align: left;")
txtstream.WriteLine("    white-Space: nowrap;")
txtstream.WriteLine(" }")
txtstream.WriteLine("div")
```

```
txtstream.WriteLine("")
txtstream.WriteLine("    BORDER-RIGHT: #999999 3px solid;")
txtstream.WriteLine("    PADDING-RIGHT: 6px;")
txtstream.WriteLine("    PADDING-LEFT: 6px;")
txtstream.WriteLine("    FONT-WEIGHT: Normal;")
txtstream.WriteLine("    PADDING-BOTTOM: 6px;")
txtstream.WriteLine("    COLOR: white;")
txtstream.WriteLine("    PADDING-TOP: 6px;")
txtstream.WriteLine("    BORDER-BOTTOM: #999 1px solid;")
txtstream.WriteLine("    BACKGROUND-COLOR: navy;")
txtstream.WriteLine("     FONT-FAMILY: font-family: Cambria,
serif;")
txtstream.WriteLine("    FONT-SIZE: 10px;")
txtstream.WriteLine("    text-align: left;")
txtstream.WriteLine("    white-Space: nowrap;")
txtstream.WriteLine(" }")
txtstream.WriteLine("span")
txtstream.WriteLine("")
txtstream.WriteLine("    BORDER-RIGHT: #999999 3px solid;")
txtstream.WriteLine("    PADDING-RIGHT: 3px;")
txtstream.WriteLine("    PADDING-LEFT: 3px;")
txtstream.WriteLine("    FONT-WEIGHT: Normal;")
txtstream.WriteLine("    PADDING-BOTTOM: 3px;")
txtstream.WriteLine("    COLOR: white;")
txtstream.WriteLine("    PADDING-TOP: 3px;")
txtstream.WriteLine("    BORDER-BOTTOM: #999 1px solid;")
txtstream.WriteLine("    BACKGROUND-COLOR: navy;")
txtstream.WriteLine("     FONT-FAMILY: font-family: Cambria,
serif;")
txtstream.WriteLine("    FONT-SIZE: 10px;")
txtstream.WriteLine("    text-align: left;")
txtstream.WriteLine("    white-Space: nowrap;")
```

```
txtstream.WriteLine("    display:inline-block;")
txtstream.WriteLine("    width: 100%;")
txtstream.WriteLine(" }")
txtstream.WriteLine("textarea")
txtstream.WriteLine(""")
txtstream.WriteLine("    BORDER-RIGHT: #999999 3px solid;")
txtstream.WriteLine("    PADDING-RIGHT: 3px;")
txtstream.WriteLine("    PADDING-LEFT: 3px;")
txtstream.WriteLine("    FONT-WEIGHT: Normal;")
txtstream.WriteLine("    PADDING-BOTTOM: 3px;")
txtstream.WriteLine("    COLOR: white;")
txtstream.WriteLine("    PADDING-TOP: 3px;")
txtstream.WriteLine("    BORDER-BOTTOM: #999 1px solid;")
txtstream.WriteLine("    BACKGROUND-COLOR: navy;")
txtstream.WriteLine("    FONT-FAMILY: font-family: Cambria, serif;")
txtstream.WriteLine("    FONT-SIZE: 10px;")
txtstream.WriteLine("    text-align: left;")
txtstream.WriteLine("    white-Space: nowrap;")
txtstream.WriteLine("    width: 100%;")
txtstream.WriteLine(" }")
txtstream.WriteLine("select")
txtstream.WriteLine(""")
txtstream.WriteLine("    BORDER-RIGHT: #999999 3px solid;")
txtstream.WriteLine("    PADDING-RIGHT: 6px;")
txtstream.WriteLine("    PADDING-LEFT: 6px;")
txtstream.WriteLine("    FONT-WEIGHT: Normal;")
txtstream.WriteLine("    PADDING-BOTTOM: 6px;")
txtstream.WriteLine("    COLOR: white;")
txtstream.WriteLine("    PADDING-TOP: 6px;")
txtstream.WriteLine("    BORDER-BOTTOM: #999 1px solid;")
txtstream.WriteLine("    BACKGROUND-COLOR: navy;")
```

```
txtstream.WriteLine("    FONT-FAMILY: font-family: Cambria,
serif;")
txtstream.WriteLine("   FONT-SIZE: 10px;")
txtstream.WriteLine("   text-align: left;")
txtstream.WriteLine("   white-Space: nowrap;")
txtstream.WriteLine("   width: 100%;")
txtstream.WriteLine(" }")
txtstream.WriteLine("input")
txtstream.WriteLine("")
txtstream.WriteLine("   BORDER-RIGHT: #999999 3px solid;")
txtstream.WriteLine("   PADDING-RIGHT: 3px;")
txtstream.WriteLine("   PADDING-LEFT: 3px;")
txtstream.WriteLine("   FONT-WEIGHT: Bold;")
txtstream.WriteLine("   PADDING-BOTTOM: 3px;")
txtstream.WriteLine("   COLOR: white;")
txtstream.WriteLine("   PADDING-TOP: 3px;")
txtstream.WriteLine("   BORDER-BOTTOM: #999 1px solid;")
txtstream.WriteLine("   BACKGROUND-COLOR: navy;")
txtstream.WriteLine("    FONT-FAMILY: font-family: Cambria,
serif;")
txtstream.WriteLine("   FONT-SIZE: 12px;")
txtstream.WriteLine("   text-align: left;")
txtstream.WriteLine("   display:table-cell;")
txtstream.WriteLine("   white-Space: nowrap;")
txtstream.WriteLine("   width: 100%;")
txtstream.WriteLine(" }")
txtstream.WriteLine("h1 ")
txtstream.WriteLine("color: antiquewhite;")
txtstream.WriteLine("text-shadow: 1px 1px 1px black;")
txtstream.WriteLine("padding: 3px;")
txtstream.WriteLine("text-align: center;")
```

txtstream.WriteLine("box-shadow: inSet   2px   2px   5px rgba(0,0,0,0.5), inSet -2px -2px 5px rgba(255,255,255,0.5);")

txtstream.WriteLine(" }")

txtstream.WriteLine("</style>")

SHADOW BOX

txtstream.WriteLine("<style type='text/css'>")

txtstream.WriteLine("body")

txtstream.WriteLine("")

txtstream.WriteLine("   PADDING RIGHT: 0px;")

txtstream.WriteLine("   PADDING-LEFT: 0px;")

txtstream.WriteLine("   PADDING-BOTTOM: 0px;")

txtstream.WriteLine("   MARGIN: 0px;")

txtstream.WriteLine("   COLOR: #333;")

txtstream.WriteLine("   PADDING-TOP: 0px;")

txtstream.WriteLine("   FONT-FAMILY: verdana,   arial, helvetica, sans-serif;")

txtstream.WriteLine(" }")

txtstream.WriteLine("table")

txtstream.WriteLine("")

txtstream.WriteLine("   BORDER-RIGHT: #999999 1px solid;")

txtstream.WriteLine("   PADDING-RIGHT: 1px;")

txtstream.WriteLine("   PADDING-LEFT: 1px;")

txtstream.WriteLine("   PADDING-BOTTOM: 1px;")

txtstream.WriteLine("   LINE-HEIGHT: 8px;")

txtstream.WriteLine("   PADDING-TOP: 1px;")

txtstream.WriteLine("   BORDER-BOTTOM: #999 1px solid;")

txtstream.WriteLine("   BACKGROUND-COLOR: #eeeeee;")

txtstream.WriteLine("   filter:progid:DXImageTransform.Microsoft.Shadow(color='silver', Direction=135, Strength=16)")

```
txtstream.WriteLine(" }")
txtstream.WriteLine("th")
txtstream.WriteLine(""")
txtstream.WriteLine("    BORDER-RIGHT: #999999 3px solid;")
txtstream.WriteLine("    PADDING-RIGHT: 6px;")
txtstream.WriteLine("    PADDING-LEFT: 6px;")
txtstream.WriteLine("    FONT-WEIGHT: Bold;")
txtstream.WriteLine("    FONT-SIZE: 14px;")
txtstream.WriteLine("    PADDING-BOTTOM: 6px;")
txtstream.WriteLine("    COLOR: darkred;")
txtstream.WriteLine("    LINE-HEIGHT: 14px;")
txtstream.WriteLine("    PADDING-TOP: 6px;")
txtstream.WriteLine("    BORDER-BOTTOM: #999 1px solid;")
txtstream.WriteLine("    BACKGROUND-COLOR: #eeeeee;")
txtstream.WriteLine("    FONT-FAMILY: font-family: Cambria,
serif;")
txtstream.WriteLine("    FONT-SIZE: 12px;")
txtstream.WriteLine("    text-align: left;")
txtstream.WriteLine("    white-Space: nowrap;")
txtstream.WriteLine(" }")
txtstream.WriteLine(".th")
txtstream.WriteLine(""")
txtstream.WriteLine("    BORDER-RIGHT: #999999 2px solid;")
txtstream.WriteLine("    PADDING-RIGHT: 6px;")
txtstream.WriteLine("    PADDING-LEFT: 6px;")
txtstream.WriteLine("    FONT-WEIGHT: Bold;")
txtstream.WriteLine("    PADDING-BOTTOM: 6px;")
txtstream.WriteLine("    COLOR: black;")
txtstream.WriteLine("    PADDING-TOP: 6px;")
txtstream.WriteLine("    BORDER-BOTTOM: #999 2px solid;")
txtstream.WriteLine("    BACKGROUND-COLOR: #eeeeee;")
```

txtstream.WriteLine("   FONT-FAMILY: font-family: Cambria, serif;")
txtstream.WriteLine("   FONT-SIZE: 10px;")
txtstream.WriteLine("   text-align: right;")
txtstream.WriteLine("   white-Space: nowrap;")
txtstream.WriteLine(" }")
txtstream.WriteLine("td")
txtstream.WriteLine(""")
txtstream.WriteLine("   BORDER-RIGHT: #999999 3px solid;")
txtstream.WriteLine("   PADDING-RIGHT: 6px;")
txtstream.WriteLine("   PADDING-LEFT: 6px;")
txtstream.WriteLine("   FONT-WEIGHT: Normal;")
txtstream.WriteLine("   PADDING-BOTTOM: 6px;")
txtstream.WriteLine("   COLOR: navy;")
txtstream.WriteLine("   LINE-HEIGHT: 14px;")
txtstream.WriteLine("   PADDING-TOP: 6px;")
txtstream.WriteLine("   BORDER-BOTTOM: #999 1px solid;")
txtstream.WriteLine("   BACKGROUND-COLOR: #eeeeee;")
txtstream.WriteLine("   FONT-FAMILY: font-family: Cambria, serif;")
txtstream.WriteLine("   FONT-SIZE: 12px;")
txtstream.WriteLine("   text-align: left;")
txtstream.WriteLine("   white-Space: nowrap;")
txtstream.WriteLine(" }")
txtstream.WriteLine("div")
txtstream.WriteLine(""")
txtstream.WriteLine("   BORDER-RIGHT: #999999 3px solid;")
txtstream.WriteLine("   PADDING-RIGHT: 6px;")
txtstream.WriteLine("   PADDING-LEFT: 6px;")
txtstream.WriteLine("   FONT-WEIGHT: Normal;")
txtstream.WriteLine("   PADDING-BOTTOM: 6px;")
txtstream.WriteLine("   COLOR: white;")

```
txtstream.WriteLine("    PADDING-TOP: 6px;")
txtstream.WriteLine("    BORDER-BOTTOM: #999 1px solid;")
txtstream.WriteLine("    BACKGROUND-COLOR: navy;")
txtstream.WriteLine("      FONT-FAMILY: font-family: Cambria,
serif;")
txtstream.WriteLine("    FONT-SIZE: 10px;")
txtstream.WriteLine("    text-align: left;")
txtstream.WriteLine("    white-Space: nowrap;")
txtstream.WriteLine(" }")
txtstream.WriteLine("span")
txtstream.WriteLine(""")
txtstream.WriteLine("    BORDER-RIGHT: #999999 3px solid;")
txtstream.WriteLine("    PADDING-RIGHT: 3px;")
txtstream.WriteLine("    PADDING-LEFT: 3px;")
txtstream.WriteLine("    FONT-WEIGHT: Normal;")
txtstream.WriteLine("    PADDING-BOTTOM: 3px;")
txtstream.WriteLine("    COLOR: white;")
txtstream.WriteLine("    PADDING-TOP: 3px;")
txtstream.WriteLine("    BORDER-BOTTOM: #999 1px solid;")
txtstream.WriteLine("    BACKGROUND-COLOR: navy;")
txtstream.WriteLine("      FONT-FAMILY: font-family: Cambria,
serif;")
txtstream.WriteLine("    FONT-SIZE: 10px;")
txtstream.WriteLine("    text-align: left;")
txtstream.WriteLine("    white-Space: nowrap;")
txtstream.WriteLine("    display: inline-block;")
txtstream.WriteLine("    width: 100%;")
txtstream.WriteLine(" }")
txtstream.WriteLine("textarea")
txtstream.WriteLine(""")
txtstream.WriteLine("    BORDER-RIGHT: #999999 3px solid;")
txtstream.WriteLine("    PADDING-RIGHT: 3px;")
```

```
txtstream.WriteLine("    PADDING-LEFT: 3px;")
txtstream.WriteLine("    FONT-WEIGHT: Normal;")
txtstream.WriteLine("    PADDING-BOTTOM: 3px;")
txtstream.WriteLine("    COLOR: white;")
txtstream.WriteLine("    PADDING-TOP: 3px;")
txtstream.WriteLine("    BORDER-BOTTOM: #999 1px solid;")
txtstream.WriteLine("    BACKGROUND-COLOR: navy;")
txtstream.WriteLine("      FONT-FAMILY: font-family: Cambria,
serif;")
txtstream.WriteLine("    FONT-SIZE: 10px;")
txtstream.WriteLine("    text-align: left;")
txtstream.WriteLine("    white-Space: nowrap;")
txtstream.WriteLine("    width: 100%;")
txtstream.WriteLine(" }")
txtstream.WriteLine("select")
txtstream.WriteLine(""")
txtstream.WriteLine("    BORDER-RIGHT: #999999 3px solid;")
txtstream.WriteLine("    PADDING-RIGHT: 6px;")
txtstream.WriteLine("    PADDING-LEFT: 6px;")
txtstream.WriteLine("    FONT-WEIGHT: Normal;")
txtstream.WriteLine("    PADDING-BOTTOM: 6px;")
txtstream.WriteLine("    COLOR: white;")
txtstream.WriteLine("    PADDING-TOP: 6px;")
txtstream.WriteLine("    BORDER-BOTTOM: #999 1px solid;")
txtstream.WriteLine("    BACKGROUND-COLOR: navy;")
txtstream.WriteLine("      FONT-FAMILY: font-family: Cambria,
serif;")
txtstream.WriteLine("    FONT-SIZE: 10px;")
txtstream.WriteLine("    text-align: left;")
txtstream.WriteLine("    white-Space: nowrap;")
txtstream.WriteLine("    width: 100%;")
txtstream.WriteLine(" }")
```

```
txtstream.WriteLine("input")
txtstream.WriteLine("“)
txtstream.WriteLine("    BORDER-RIGHT: #999999 3px solid;")
txtstream.WriteLine("    PADDING-RIGHT: 3px;")
txtstream.WriteLine("    PADDING-LEFT: 3px;")
txtstream.WriteLine("    FONT-WEIGHT: Bold;")
txtstream.WriteLine("    PADDING-BOTTOM: 3px;")
txtstream.WriteLine("    COLOR: white;")
txtstream.WriteLine("    PADDING-TOP: 3px;")
txtstream.WriteLine("    BORDER-BOTTOM: #999 1px solid;")
txtstream.WriteLine("    BACKGROUND-COLOR: navy;")
txtstream.WriteLine("     FONT-FAMILY: font-family: Cambria,
serif;")
txtstream.WriteLine("    FONT-SIZE: 12px;")
txtstream.WriteLine("    text-align: left;")
txtstream.WriteLine("    display: table-cell;")
txtstream.WriteLine("    white-Space: nowrap;")
txtstream.WriteLine("    width: 100%;")
txtstream.WriteLine(" }")
txtstream.WriteLine("h1 “)
txtstream.WriteLine("color: antiquewhite;")
txtstream.WriteLine("text-shadow: 1px 1px 1px black;")
txtstream.WriteLine("padding: 3px;")
txtstream.WriteLine("text-align: center;")
txtstream.WriteLine("box-shadow:   inSet   2px   2px   5px
rgba(0,0,0,0.5), inSet -2px -2px 5px rgba(255,255,255,0.5);")
txtstream.WriteLine(" }")
txtstream.WriteLine("</style>“)
```